W9-AUK-289

The
Robert J. Lurtsema
MUSICAL
Quiz Book

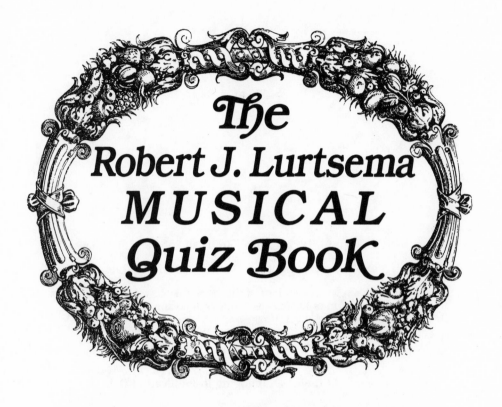

The
Robert J. Lurtsema
MUSICAL
Quiz Book

BY **Roger Kolb** & **Robert J. Lurtsema**
ILLUSTRATIONS BY **David Omar White**

The Countryman Press
WOODSTOCK, VERMONT

Text copyright © 1992 by Roger Kolb and Robert J. Lurtsema

Illustrations copyright © 1992 by David Omar White

All rights reserved. No part of this book may be reproduced
in any form or by any electronic or mechanical means
including information storage and retrieval systems without
permission in writing from the publisher, except by a
reviewer, who may quote brief passages.

Library of Congress Cataloging-in-Publication Data

Kolb, Roger, 1946–
    The Robert J. Lurtsema musical quiz book / Roger Kolb
and Robert J. Lurtsema; illustrations by David Omar White.
        p.   cm.
    Includes bibliographical references.
    ISBN 0-88150-221-9
    1. Music—Miscellanea.   I. Lurtsema, Robert J.   II. Title.
ML63.K76   1992   92-10388
780—dc20   CIP
                                        MN

Published by The Countryman Press, Inc.
Woodstock, Vermont 05091

Cover and text design by James F. Brisson

Cover drawings by David Omar White

Printed in the United States of America on recycled paper

10 9 8 7 6 5 4 3 2 1

To all who grow up with an insatiable curiosity

CONTENTS

Introduction

The process of producing a book is, by its very nature, a collaborative effort. When all the related activities are accounted for, the extent of that collaboration is astonishing. Lumber has to be made into pulp, pressed into paper, processed, cut, and bound. The book must be written, edited, proofed, printed, and presented. In addition to the people who produce all of this, many more provide the pens, pencils, word processors, and printing mechanisms. Often a book such as this one relies on many other books, which of course had to go through the same process. Then add to this the legions of people involved in advertising, marketing, distribution, and sales and you have an enormous army of individuals involved in the production of a single book.

As a multi-author effort, this book is even more of a collaboration. Roger Kolb came to me with the idea of putting together a book that would combine musical anecdotes, quizzes, and cartoons. David Omar White, as an artist and political satirist, was a natural choice to illustrate the book.

As a librarian, Roger was ideally suited to the meticulous research that was required. He was assisted by MIT's music librarians Nina Davis-Millis, Christie Moore, and Forrest Larson, as well as the music staff of the Boston Public Library. Larry Hamberlin, Ted Wood, Peter Silberman, George Koch, Ellen Duranceau, Don Robinson, Steve Skuce, Jim and Marcie Rosenberg, and Harry Ellis Dickson helped with a variety of problems related to the text.

Elizabeth Northrup's secretarial skills and organizational ability kept things moving along in high spirits, and The Countryman Press stirred the mix with boundless enthusiasm and encouragement.

From the outset, it was an evolutionary process involving consultation, confrontation, consideration, and compromise. Many hands do not necessarily make lighter work, nor does it mean that the work will take less time. From its inception, this book took almost two years to complete. Since there were many periods of inactivity while one or the other of us waited for a project to be finished, I was actually able to write another book, *A Pocketful of Verse*, which was started after this book was begun and published by Parnassus Imprints, before this book was completed, which means this is either my first or second book.

The same kind of thing happens in music. A composer writes a piano concerto and before it gets published, he writes another which is published as #1. Then his first concerto is published as #2. Now I could finish that anecdote by revealing that this is what happened with Beethoven, Liszt, and Chopin or I could leave out the names of the composers and provide only the clues that would help you guess their identities. Then it would be a quiz rather than an anecdote. This book has an abundance of both.

A quiz book, by its very nature, is meant to provide a challenge and, at the same time, an opportunity for learning. Working on this book has certainly done that for us and it is my sincere wish that it will do the same for you.

Robert J. Lurtsema

1
Conductors and Orchestras

Lets begin with a little history. *Very* little. It concerns the symphony orchestra—that splendid gang of scrapers, tooters, and bangers for whom people build such places as Symphony and Severance halls.

We have to go back to the seventeenth century and Louis XIV. For the Sun King, everything had to be magnificent, a splendor that extended also to his music. Not content with his fiddlers three or however many string players he had, His Majesty added two oboes and a bassoon. Courts in Germany and Austria, refusing to be outdone, were soon following the king's suit. Eventually, amateurs who had been making music together whenever the spirit moved them started scheduling regular concerts and selling subscriptions. As orchestras grew in size and repertoire, more and more folks said that their hometowns needed one to show that they had culturally arrived. Londoners, New Yorkers, and the Viennese could even boast later on that they were supporting not one but two at the same time.

Which of these is the seating plan used by most of today's symphony orchestras?

QUESTION

1

A

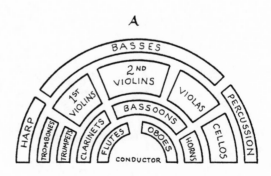

3

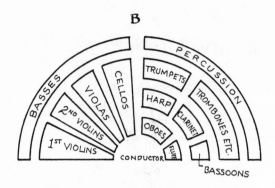

B

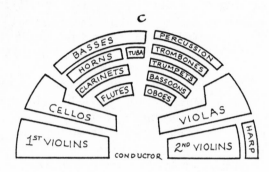

C

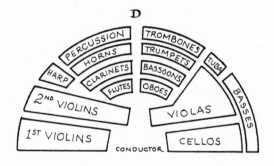

D

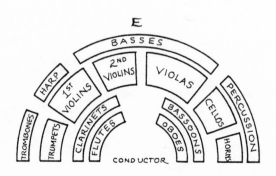

E

4

The Bingo Comee Traveling All-Star Music Circus
Aka the Boston Symphony Orchestra

Call It the Bingo Comee
Traveling All-Star Music Circus

So familiar has the orchestra become since the heyday of Haydn that the notion that anyone in the civilized world could be ignorant of what it does and how it does it seems strange. But that is what Fred Comee found out in the 1880s in a city in central New York as the assistant manager of the touring Boston Symphony Orchestra. No sooner had the BSO pulled into that Empire State town than he did what managers usually do straightaway: he went to the box office to check on advance ticket receipts. The advance sale was slack, prompting Comee to turn to the theater manager in dismay.

"When do you parade?" asked the gentleman.

"Parade?" echoed the puzzled Comee.

"Sure. Don't your troupe always parade before the show? You won't do business without it."

We can only conjecture about what the BSO might have chosen for parade music. Neither "The Darktown Strutters' Ball" nor "The South Rampart Street Parade" had yet been written. "When the Saints Go Marching In" was available. That might have been an appropriate choice, or maybe a rousing circus march.

Comee, as an assistant orchestra manager, was used to wearing many hats. But not a drum major's!

One of the following statements is false. Which one?

A. In the eighteenth century, orchestras were led by the first violinist waving his bow or by a keyboard soloist directing with his hands.

B. The baton was introduced by Felix Mendelssohn in 1849.

C. Trumpets and French horns in the orchestras of Beethoven's day were valveless; valves for those intruments were introduced around the time of his death in 1827.

D. The short-lived Symphony of the Air, the name for the former Toscanini-led NBC Symphony, made a recording or two in the fifties without a conductor.

E. An example of a contemporary ensemble that performs without a conductor is the Orpheus Chamber Orchestra.

Cracking under Pressure

In 1911, twelve years before taking over as the music director of the Boston Symphony Orchestra, Serge Koussevitzky was in Saint Petersburg, Russia, to lead his orchestra in the eagerly awaited world premiere of Alexander Scriabin's tone poem *Prometheus*. Excitement was intense in the orchestra as everyone was concerned about playing his part correctly. Most concerned of all was an overwrought percussionist whose responsibility was to perform a stroke on a gong at a climactic moment. Worried that he might miss his cue amid the complexity and volume of Scriabin's score, he arranged for the musician beside him to deliver a pair of signals in the form of a nod of the head followed by a downward swishing of the arm. Regrettably, at the public rehearsal, the percussionist became confused in the din and, instead of hitting the gong, brought his mallet down with immense force on his neighbor's noggin. The sound not of a gong, but of a bloodcurdling scream soared from the Scriabin-esque tumult.

A Promethean Rehearsal Scene
"Not me, dummy, the gong!"

A Musical Rube

Koussevitzky took his orchestra all over Russia, even penetrating regions in which musical organizations such as his were rarely seen. A concert in southeastern Russia attracted a good-natured farmer who, as far as music was concerned, was obviously naïve. As he sat in the first row, he became intrigued as he watched the trombonist pushing out and pulling in the trombone slide. To the farmer, it appeared that the musician waas trying to separate the two parts of his instrument, and finding it impossible. At intermission, the farmer rushed over to the musician, took the trombone, and with one herculean effort, pulled the instrument apart. He smiled and bowed, handed the musician the two parts of the trombone, and said in effect, "It's all yours now, sir."

One of the following statements about Koussevitzky is false. Which one?

QUESTION
3

A. It was Koussevitzky who asked Maurice Ravel to orchestrate Mussorgsky's *Pictures at an Exhibition.*

B. A lifelong champion of modern music, Koussevitzky commissioned new works from Stravinsky, Bartok, Ravel, Hindemith, Prokofiev, Roussel, and many American composers.

C. The idea of having summertime concerts in western Massachusetts was Koussevitzky's.

D. Koussevitzky founded the Berkshire Music Center, a school for training musicians for positions of leadership in the music world.

E. One of Koussevitzky's students in conducting at Tanglewood was Leonard Bernstein.

The French Defection

French orchestra musicians were so poorly paid early in this century that they were allowed to find substitutes for themselves whenever higher fees beckoned elsewhere. With a concert coming up in Paris, Koussevitzky was at his wit's end coping with all of the defections among his forces. Noticing that the piccolo player had stayed with him throughout, Koussevitzky thanked him for his loyalty at the dress rehearsal saying, "I am so glad to see that at least you have remained with me all the time."

"Ah, monsieur," the other responded, "but I shall not be here tomorrow for the performance."

Watch Out for Low-Flying Bows

Koussevitzky figured in another unprogrammed incident, this one involving a fiddle player with the Boston Symphony. During a concert at Sanders Theater in Cambridge, BSO violinist Richard Lehner's bow flew out of his hands and landed in the lap of a woman in the first row. Koussevitzky didn't see it. His gaze was fixed elsewhere, allowing the embarrassed but unflappable Lehner to keep his hands moving rapidly, drawing an imaginary bow across the body of his violin. A few measures later, when Koussevitzky turned to the other side of the orchestra, the lady tactfully returned the bow to the clever violinist.

Not a Transparent Score

Needless to say, something is less likely to go wrong when an orchestra is performing a piece it has played many times than when the piece is a strange-sounding contemporary work or an older item not in the repertory. One afternoon, Koussevitzky and the Boston

Richard Lehner's Airborne Bow
Throwing one's all into the music

Symphony had just finished the rehearsal of a complex new work during which almost everyone, including the conductor, had got lost. The second oboist, Jean Devergie, then leaned over to the first-desk player, Fernand Gillet, and asked him what they were scheduled to play next. When Gillet showed him his part for the next piece, Devergie exclaimed, "My God! I just played it!"

Which *one* of the following statements about the Boston Symphony Orchestra is false?

A. The Boston Symphony Orchestra was founded in 1881 by Henry Higginson, who remained its sole director until almost the day of his death in 1919.

B. The Boston Symphony's first conductor was a singer, George Henschel, who as a recitalist often performed duets with his wife.

C. The Boston Symphony's music director during the First World War, Karl Muck, was arrested as an enemy alien, after which the orchestra had a couple of French conductors before the appointment of Koussevitzky.

D. The conductor at the raucous world premiere in Paris of Stravinsky's *Rite of Spring* on May 29, 1913, was future BSO music director Pierre Monteux.

E. The Boston Symphony was one of the first major orchestras in America to unionize.

Franck Who?

Any number of writers have commented that for many musicians music is their whole life, nothing outside of it having much reality. The nineteenth-century composer Luigi Arditi, it is said, was talking to someone who casually mentioned the name Shakespeare. "Who?" asked Arditi. "You know, *Shakespeare*," said the other, startled, "the author of *Othello*." "Ah, yes," exclaimed Arditi triumphantly, "Shakespeare *the librettist*."

Many years later, a similar exchange involved Jean Le Franc, the soft-spoken, retiring first violinist of the Boston Symphony. Before a performance in Pittsburgh, there was a stir among the players when word swept through the orchestra that Frank Sinatra was in the audience. When Ol' Blue Eyes came backstage during the intermission, Le Franc turned in puzzlement to a fellow musician and said "*Mais oui*, I know the Franck Sonata, but who is this man?"

An Interpretation of Rare Allure

On a Thursday evening, around the time that James Michael Curley was first elected mayor of Boston, a rally on his behalf was held in Symphony Hall. As part of the festivities, helium-filled balloons were released, which then floated up to the ceiling, where they remained overnight. With so little time before the matinee, the decision was made to leave then there. No sooner had the orchestra begun to play that afternoon than the balloons began slowly to descend, hovering above the audience. Eventually, they drifted toward the musicians, where they were drawn to the brass like iron filings to a magnet.

An Interpretation of Rare Allure
Too bad Up, Up, and Away *hadn't been written yet*

Match the American Symphony Orchestra with its current music director.

Cleveland – A   1 – Daniel Barenboim

Chicago – B   2 – Herbert Blomstedt

Dallas – C   3 – Christoph von Dohnányi

Philadelphia – D   4 – Eduardo Mata

San Francisco – E   5 – Riccardo Muti

Seattle – F   6 – Gerard Schwarz

Saint Louis – G   7 – Leonard Slatkin

In the Spirit of Things

Benny Fiedler, uncle of Arthur Fiedler, was a long-time string player with the Boston Symphony. The tenure of Benny, an acid wit, overlapped that of the orchestra's present-day memoirist, violinist Harry

Ellis Dickson. In his book about Koussevitzky and the Boston Symphony, *Gentlemen, More Dolce Please,* Dickson recalls a performance under Koussevitzky of Tchaikovsky's *Pathétique* Symphony that squeezed every last drop of emotion out of that melancholy work. Koussevitzky loved the piece; he identified with it so strongly that he probably came to believe he had composed it himself. On this particular occasion, as the low strings brought the work to its tragic close, there wasn't a dry eye in Symphony Hall. The audience was in tears. Koussevitzky was in tears. The ushers were in tears. Everyone in the orchestra was in tears. Everyone, that is, except Benny, who sat staring downward with a strange look on his face. Finally, he looked up slowly at Harry and said, "Dickson, do you like my new shoes?"

Benny Fiedler and Harry Ellis Dickson
An urgent question is asked

Which *one* of the following statements about Arthur Fiedler and the Boston Pops is false?

A. The Boston Pops may be defined as the Boston Symphony Orchestra minus its first-desk players and music director.

B. The Boston Pops was founded by Arthur Fiedler.

C. The idea for having free concerts on the Charles River Esplanade was Fiedler's.

D. Before marrying in middle age, Fiedler was a ladies' man who had many love affairs, including one with stage and film actress Jeanne Eagels.

E. In the early fifties, the Pops under Fiedler had a pair of hit records, *Jalousie* by Jacob Gade and *Blue Tango* by Leroy Anderson.

A Marvelously Malleable, Plastic, Fantastic Maestro

Walter Damrosch, conductor of the New York Symphony Orchestra from the 1880s to 1927, was one of the most resourceful conductors in music history. To him, the show had to go on. He was able to conduct his orchestra under the most difficult conditions. During a winter concert in Rochester, New York, a blizzard literally tore the roof off the stage, creating a veritable witches' sabbath of things flapping and banging. Damrosch didn't care. He just kept on calmly conducting Debussy's *Afternoon of a Faun* to its quiet conclusion and then turned solemnly as he always did to acknowledge the applause of an appreciative audience.

On another occasion, Damrosch and his musicians were in midconcert when a bolt of lightning from an electrical storm outside struck the generator and plunged the auditorium into total darkness. Sensing growing panic amid the increasingly fearsome tempest, the resourceful conductor called out to his first trombonist to begin the "Coronation March" from *The Prophet*. The orchestra performed Meyerbeer's march entirely in the dark, thereby averting a stampede.

Perhaps Damrosch's all-time masterpiece of adjusting to circumstances on tour occured when the lengthy applause following the first piece on the program, the *Tannhäuser* Overture, put the orchestra in danger of missing its train out of town. The last piece was

Walter Damrosch in Rochester
A sensitively shaded reading of Debussy's Afternoon of a Faun

Tchaikovsky's *Pathétique* Symphony, which concludes with a long and lugubrious adagio. Midway through the movement, it became obvious that the Night Owl was going to leave without the orchestra unless something was done. Thirty minutes to go and there they were, mired in Tchaikovsky's self-pity. Damrosch removed his watch from his pocket and looked at it pensively. Steadily, his tempo gained speed. The adagio became an allegro. The allegro became a vivace. The poignance of the Russian master's swan song was reduced to a tornado of emotional mishmash. Climaxes and carefully sculpted phrases went by breathlessly, like a videocassette of *Casablanca* on fast forward. To the orchestra's dismay, it turned out that the audience liked Tchaikovsky any way it could get him, applauding so long at the end that it nearly undid all the good that was done. But the day was saved. Seventy or eighty members of the New York Symphony, sweating and panting, tossed their instruments to waiting aides and porters and jumped onto the rear of the train as it slowly pulled out of the station.

Grubbiness Is Just A Thing Called Joe

Whenever the Damrosch-led New York Symphony went on tour around the country, the musicians, many of them foreign-born, felt that the train protected them from the savageries of the young American nation. Everyone would become highly protective of his suitcase, which gave him a sense of security, and would try to pack as many luxuries inside of it as space would allow. The musician who probably had the most room for them was a violinist whom we will call Joe Ullman. Joe was a dyed-in-the-wool conservative who disliked change in any form, including change of clothing. Unlike many of his fellows, he was a married man, wed to a wealthy woman of whose financial status he was exceptionally proud. He also took great pride in his personal appearance, which he and others believed to resemble Beethoven's. Marriage had failed to change Joe's conservatism; he always looked like a walking statue of Beethoven, wrapped up in a big overcoat topped by a hat. Just be-

Joe Ullman's Beethovenian Bearing
But did Ludwig wear fruit on his hat?

fore the orchestra would embark on a tour, his wife would buy Joe a new set of clothes, from suit down to tie and socks, and put an overcoat and hat on him. The suit never came off him—*never*. The overcoat and hat were shed only at the last second before concerts. Joe ate in the overcoat and hat. Joe slept in the overcoat and hat. And Joe was the marvel of all the New York Symphony Orchestra when he shaved in overcoat and hat. Needless to say, after a while Joe's overcoat acquired so much color in the form of dried egg yolk, tomato sauce, and cigar ash that it resembled a middle-period Kandinsky. Damrosch would look at the coat and say to the other men as though reading a ship's log, "Gentlemen, I see that the tour is almost over."

Joe was a Silesian in an orchestra whose membership was decidedly cosmopolitan. One day, he was dining—in overcoat and hat, of course—when a French oboe player passed behind him and gently deposited a banana peel on the brim of his chapeau. A chain reaction was then set in motion. A number of other musicians finished eating and walked behind the eccentric violinist, placing whatever was left of their meals—eggshells, lettuce leaves, cigar butts—on top of Joe's head. Eventually, Joe got up, proudly affected a stern Beethovenian countenance, and strode out of the dining room, passing Damrosch on the way. "Good evening, Ullman," said the conductor without batting an eye. Meanwhile a couple of German musicians had caught sight of all this and had become hostile at this slur upon Central European masculinity. One of them went over to Joe and, slowly lifting the hat, flung its contents at the French oboe player. As a fracas began to take shape, Jimmy, the orchestra's burly baggage man, threw himself between the opposing factions, thereby averting an international incident.

QUESTION
7 | **Which *two* of the following are false?**

A. Damrosch's New York Symphony commissioned Gershwin's Concerto in F, and it was Damrosch who exclaimed to the audience after leading the premiere of Copland's *Organ* Symphony: "If a young man at the age of twenty-three can write a symphony like that, in five years he will be ready to commit murder!"

B. The formal name of the New York Philharmonic is "The Philharmonic-Symphony Society Orchestra of New York," which it assumed in 1928 when it merged with Damrosch's New York Symphony Society.

16

c. Lured to this country by a fabulous salary offer from the Metropolitan Opera, Gustav Mahler led the Met orchestra and the New York Philharmonic for two seasons each.

d. At different times, Arturo Toscanini led the Met's orchestra and the NBC Symphony, but never the New York Philharmonic; the Philharmonic, it is believed, feared his volcanic temper.

e. Kurt Masur and Klaus Tennstedt recently were named music directors of the New York and Berlin Philharmonic Orchestras, respectively.

Fake Out

The New York Philharmonic gave a concert in the 1940s in White Plains, New York, about half an hour north of the city by rail. The last train left White Plains at eleven o'clock, meaning that if the orchestra missed the train, they would have to wait until morning. To save time, conductor Artur Rodzinski decided to put "The Star-Spangled Banner" at the end of the concert instead of the beginning. (The national anthem was required at all concerts in those days.) Because anthems were not applauded, he figured that the orchestra would be able to pack up right away at the concert's conclusion, instead of having to wait around to acknowledge applause. It so happened that the opening piece on the program was Beethoven's *Egmont* Overture, whose first note, like the national anthem's, is an F. When it was sounded, six thousand people rose from their seats. Rodzinski said his thoughts ran to many things, including whether he had remembered to put on his pants.

Paging Tinker Bell

Leonard Bernstein was rehearsing the New York Philharmonic for a reading of Mendelssohn's sprightly *Midsummer Night's Dream*, with its suggestion of frisky elves, satyrs, and nymphs gamboling about an enchanted glade. No matter how hard he explained, exhorted, and cajoled, Bernstein couldn't get his group to capture the spirit of anything more puckish than a bull elephant. Finally, he put down his baton and gave it to them straight. "What this orchestra needs," he said, "is more fairies."

The Vision Of Leonard Bernstein
What every performance of A Midsummer Night's Dream *needs*

A Pressing Engagement

For one of his concerts in his 1958 Musica Viva series, conductor John Pritchard of the Royal Philharmonic scheduled the orchestral suite from Berg's opera *Lulu*, written when it was *de rigeur* among German intellectuals to act depressed, disillusioned, and demented. Sometimes when the piece is performed, a soprano aria is included with a backstage shriek from the heroine. Pritchard decided to eliminate the aria but to retain the scream. Any woman would have sufficed, but Pritchard for some reason decided to hire a gorgeous actress. The responsibility of young assistant conductor Zubin Mehta was to stand backstage and give the woman her cue after the music had reached its climax.

At the concert, the music built to its climax, stopped, and—no scream. It is difficult for a woman to scream when her mouth is being pressed into service for another purpose.

Later on, to excuse his conduct, the future New York Philharmonic maestro said, "The woman was *so beautiful!*"

Which *one* of the following statements about Leonard Bernstein is false?

A. In 1958 Bernstein became the first American-born music director of the New York Philharmonic.

B. Bernstein bestowed considerable respectability upon popular music both as a Broadway composer and as the host of a TV special in the 1960s in which he expressed a taste for a number of recent pop songs.

C. A composer to whom Bernstein felt especially close was Gustav Mahler.

D. A biography of Bernstein by Joan Peyser created a considerable stir when it was published in 1987 because it alleged that Bernstein was gay.

Mehta and the Actress
Theirs was a Lulu *of a performance*

E. Composer Pierre Boulez was named music director of the New York Philharmonic in the early seventies to introduce audiences to modern music; his predecessor, Bernstein, played very little of it.

Breaking with old Taboos

A superstition among musicians holds that it is bad to have sex before a concert. Andre Kostelanetz wasn't sure about this, so he decided to ask his more experienced friend Leopold Stokowski how he felt about it. Stokowski told him without hesitation, "It all depends on the woman."

Ring Out the Old

Stokowski is said to have had a condescending attitude toward older musicians, evidently believing that when someone got beyond a certain age, he was no longer capable of playing with a big-league orchestra. Apparently he also thought that the ravages of time did not affect conductors, inasmuch as he worked right up to his own death in 1977 at the age of ninety-five.

In the late fifties, an unexpected resignation left the Symphony of the Air without a first trumpet, a deficiency rendered doubly acute by the forthcoming performance of an American piece with difficult solo passages for that instrument. Hired to fill the post was a musician of vast experience, an absolutely world-class trumpeter who, as first chair with the NBC Symphony, had helped Toscanini realize many a remarkable performance. When Stokowski, who was to conduct the American piece, heard who had been appointed, he was dismayed. He had had the man in Philadelphia in the twenties. That was thirty years ago, and now the man was old, *too* old. "This is not good news," said Stokowski over and over to the orchestra's manager, Jerome Toobin.

To dismiss the man would have stirred up a hornet's nest in the union, and so, with fingers crossed, everyone stood pat and hoped for the best. At the first rehearsal of the American piece Stokowski laid down his baton a few measures into the first solo passage to tell the new first trumpet that he was not satisfied with his playing. Trumpet was too loud. They began again. They stopped again. Trumpet was too soft. They resumed. Trumpet, you are not up to tempo, please count. Trumpet, trumpet, trumpet was the leitmotif.

At first the musician, known for his low boiling point, remained

An All-Too-Memorable Stokowski Rehearsal
He was too loud, too soft, too fast, and too slow—
sometimes at the same time

quiet and patient, giving every indication of attempting to follow the maestro's orders. Eventually, he took the hint, realizing that Stokowski's objections to him were not ones relating to loud and soft, slow and fast. The blowup was frightful.

"Look, you goddamned has-been," the musician erupted, "who the hell do you think you are?"

Strings, woodwinds, brass, percussion, symphony officers, mice in the walls—everyone and everything froze.

"This isn't Philadelphia thirty years ago!" he continued. "And you're nobody. You has-been! Wake up; you're nobody!"

No, not everyone froze. One person remained relaxed—Stokowski. Unfazed, he just sat on the stool he always kept behind himself at rehearsals, lazily swinging his leg against it. He waved one hand at the trumpeter in a gesture of dismissal, saying, "Good aftahnoon, suh. Good aftahnoon, suh."

More members of the tableau became unfrozen when the personnel manager sped over to the trumpeter and carried him off, the latter yelling innumerable imprecations. Stokowski beckoned to Toobin, the manager, who had sunk so low in his chair that he felt he'd fallen into a trench. Apprehensively, Toobin walked over to the high chair.

"Mr. Too-been," Stokowski said sweetly, "can you get that wahn-dah-fool player who did Wagner with us? You know, the big man . . ."

And thus spoke the maestro as he sat there on that high stool casually swinging his leg. The man they called Stoki.

QUESTION
9

One of the following statements about Leopold Stokowski is mostly or entirely false. Which one?

A. As with his contemporary Toscanini, Stokowski played and recorded relatively little music composed after the First World War.

B. During his long professional life, Stokowski heard a stubborn rumor that he was born Leo Stokes and that he had lengthened his name in order to seem more culturally remote and mysterious.

C. In later years Stokowski always lied about his age by five years and was very sensitive on the subject, once exploding during an aborted radio interview when the announcer referred to his correct natal year, 1882.

D. Stokowski, who usually conducted without a baton and who was famous for his graceful hands, was particular about his appearance and would not allow the publication of unauthorized, candid photographs of himself.

E. Born into poverty, Stokowski had three wives, all of them wealthy, and between two of his marriages had a love affair with Greta Garbo.

Immovable Object

Though musicians often questioned his technical competence, Sir Thomas Beecham was England's most famous and popular conductor throughout most of his adult life. No one else's talents as a conductor and recording artist were as much in demand around the world as were his.

On one of his vacations in northern England, he arrived without notification at his usual hotel, where he was told that his favorite room had been taken.

Beecham, protesting that he had always had that room, requested that the manager ask its present occupant if he would move to another.

The manager replied that he could not; the gentleman in the room had already gone to bed.

Undaunted, Sir Thomas said that he would go upstairs himself and ask. He went to the door of the room, with the manager following closely behind. Roused by Beecham's knock, the guest replied in response to his request, "Certainly not, I'll do nothing of the kind."

"But," protested the manager, "this is Sir Thomas Beecham."

The guest responded, "I don't care if it's Sir Malcolm Sargent."

The Old Switcheroo

Such a strong impression did the music of Frederick Delius make on Sir Thomas Beecham that it led to a degree of espousal that might be described as a lifelong personal crusade. Not only did Beecham perform and record Delius often, but he wrote a book about him, a biography that is still, despite superficiality and inaccuracy here and there, one of the fuller treatments of the composer's life.

Once Sir Thomas was at a dinner party at which his hostess delighted him by producing a recording of Delius's *On Hearing the First Cuckoo in Spring*, saying as she put it on the phonograph that with that recording she had made a considerable number of converts for Delius. Beecham settled back awaiting the familiar strains when to his surprise he heard not Delius but Moritz Moszkowski's *Scherzo capriccioso*. The labels were reversed. Delius was on the other side.

How to Make a Guy Feel Important

Sir Landon Ronald was scheduled to conduct an orchestral piece at a Glasgow concert following two or three works to be led by an eminent maestro from across the Channel. When Sir Landon had finished, a flapper—these were the 1920s—approached him and asked for his autograph. Unhesitatingly, he produced a pencil and wrote his name down in her book. Seconds later she returned and told him that an unfortunate mistake had been made. She had thought he was the other conductor, the eminent maestro from across the Channel, and now she asked Sir Landon if she could borrow his eraser.

Name the American symphony orchestra of which the conductors in each of the following groups were once music director.

A. _____ Frederick Stock, Rafael Kubelik, Fritz Reiner, Jean Martinon, Sir Georg Solti

B. _____ Nikolai Sokoloff, Artur Rodzinski, Erich Leinsdorf, George Szell, Lorin Maazel

C. _____ Antonio Modarelli, Fritz Reiner, William Steinberg, Andre Prévin

D. _____ Pierre Monteux, Enrique Jordá, Josef Krips, Seiji Ozawa, Edo de Waart

E. _____ William Steinberg, Josef Krips, Lukas Foss, Michael Tilson Thomas, Semyon Bychkov

Anybody Can Wave a Stick

Among other things, Otto Klemperer was famous for his carelessness and absentmindedness. One day he walked into a barbershop, sat down, and was asked whether it would be a haircut or a shave that day. Abstractedly he told the man to just change the oil, please.

Klemperer, a refugee from the Third Reich, became conductor in 1933 of the Los Angeles Philharmonic. The entire German and Austrian émigré community attended his concert début. As he was receiving their congratulations in the greenroom after the concert, the orchestra began playing again. Klemperer hurried to the stage, where he found William Clark, at that time the lone underwriter of the Philharmonic, leading his forces in a rousing rendition of *The Stars and Stripes Forever* to an empty auditorium.

Oops!

For many years Italian-born Luigi Arditi, he of Shakespeare-the-librettist, conducted opera in Ireland, where, on the strength of his artistry and personality, he became genuinely loved. At the end of the first act of an Arditi-led performance of Verdi's *Ernani* in Dublin, an orange-, green-, and white-beribboned case filled with gifts for him was lowered from the ceiling. As Arditi opened the box, cries from the gallery went up for a speech. The beloved maestro complied, thanking everyone from the bottom of his heart for their

The Los Angeles Philharmonic under the direction of William Clark
What's so hard about waving a stick, anyway?

kindness and adding that he had every reason to be grateful to Dublin because it was there that he had made his first appearance in *England*.

Oscar Levant tells of an occurrence involving the home of Philadelphia's summertime orchestra, the Robin Hood Dell. To advertise a forthcoming concert and the eminent musicians participating, a gigantic banner was run across the entrance that read MITROPOULOS—FUCHS. The two names kept most of the audience chuckling for the better part of the summer.

Sound your A's. You will have the correct answer when you say "Arditi" if you are ever asked who wrote the once-popular concert aria "Il bacio." Provide answers to the following questions, all of which, like Arditi, begin with the first letter of the alphabet.

QUESTION

11

A. A_____ Pianist Emanuel or Lizzie Borden's favorite instrument.

B. A_____ > and ^ are examples, or actress Streep's specialty.

A Robin Hood Dell Announcement
Always a cause for celebration

C. A_____ Maria Callas's record label, or jockey Cordero, or Henry Travers in *It's a Wonderful Life*, for example.

D. A_____ *Trial by Jury* heroine, or nineteenth-century abolitionist Grimké.

E. A_____ Nineteenth-century Russian composer Rubinstein, or tenor Dermota, or actress Susan.

F. A_____ *Die Fledermaus* maid or nutritionist Davis.

G. A_____ English film composer John _____, known for *Tom Jones*, or the collaborator of *The Spectator*'s Sir Richard Steele.

H. A_____ Distinguished violinist and violin teacher Leopold _____, or thirties film actor Mischa.

I. A_____ "Syncopated Clock" and "Blue Tango" composer, or soprano June, or "Father Knows Best" family.

J. A_____ Handel's oratorio _____'s *Feast*, or Mr. Nevsky, or tasty brandy libation.

K. A_____ A song by Beethoven (his Opus 46), or a violin concerto in D attributed to Mozart, or the capital of South Australia, or *Guys and Dolls* spinsterhood lamenter.

L. A_____ Schumann wrote a charming one (his Opus 18), Debussy two, or 1966 comedy-spy film starring Gregory Peck and Sophia Loren.

M. A_____ Italian tempo marking that literally means "happy" or "cheerful," or an unsuccessful 1947 Broadway musical by Rodgers and Hammerstein.

N. A_____ Trumpeter Maurice, or British army officer who conspired with Benedict Arnold.

O. A_____ A suite for television by Norman Dello Joio, or what was the decisive factor in the Persian Gulf War (two words).

P. A_____ Russian pianist Vladimir whose surname sounds like the word for Eastern European Jews.

Q. A_____ *Giselle* and "O Holy Night" composer, or musicologist Carse, or Sovietologist Ulam, or eighteenth-century English architect-designer brothers Robert and James, or an ancestor of us all.

R. A_____ Conductor Kurt, or harmonica player Larry, or acting teacher Stella.

S. A_____ Russian pianist Friedheim (1859–1932), or *Shane* actress Jean, or 1981 Dudley Moore film role as an amiable inebriate.

T. A_____ A symphony by Richard Strauss, or *Heidi*'s general locale.

U. A_____ Rosalinde's *Die Fledermaus* wooer, or ninth-century Saxon king who thwarted the Danes.

V. A_____ Formal songs, usually accompanied, in an opera or oratorio, or Costa Rican premier.

W. A_____ *Sleeping Beauty* heroine, or northern lights word.

X. A_____ Penguin hangout, or the inspiration for Vaughan Williams's Seventh Symphony.

Y. A_____ Harpsichordist Newman, or pop trumpeter Ray, or nineteenth-century feminist doyenne Susan, or saintly founder of Christian monasticism.

Z. A_____ Serialism propounder Schoenberg, or English composer Malcolm, or well-known bread manufacturer known for its brick oven loaves.

2
Composers

The Food of Love

Around 1780, Joseph Haydn received a letter from a young unmarried woman phrased in language usually reserved for friends of many years' standing. Beginning the letter with "Dear, good, peerless Mr. Haydn," the lady explained that she was a captain's daughter, in love with an officer who couldn't bring himself to make the fateful Commitment. She theorized that if dear, good Mr. Haydn were to write her a beautiful melody for a song she could sing to her beloved on a particular subject dear to his heart, he would be so charmed by her performance that he would wish to shed his bachelor status right on the spot. In considerable detail she explained to Haydn why he should do this and enclosed a few ducats—all she could afford—for good measure.

She described how she, the music-loving officer, and a friend of his had been out for a stroll recently during which the officer's claims for the loyalty and intelligence of his French poodle made excessive demands on his friend's credulity. The two made a bet. The officer wagered that if he were to hide a coin under a bush and then, after walking a considerable distance from the burial site, yell, "Lost! Go find it!" to his poodle, the dog would find the coin and bring it back. Sure enough, the officer got his coin back. Only it wasn't that afternoon but the following morning that the canine showed up with it.

A passerby, it seems, had sat down under a bush to rest, spotted the coin, and pocketed it. The poodle, realizing what had happened, played up to the man, who was delighted to have acquired in the space of a few minutes both a valuable coin and a handsome pet. When the man retired at an inn that night, he removed his pants with the coin inside. The poodle immediately rolled the pants into a ball. When the cleaning lady opened the door the following morning, the dog bolted out with the man's pants in his mouth and brought them to his master.

29

This was the event the young woman wished to immortalize in song in hopes of captivating her beloved. She enclosed a poem, "The Sly and Ever-Helpful Poodle," and a stipulation that the melody contain a lot of rests, which made the amused Haydn wonder about her abilities as a singer.

Haydn composed the tune (which was published many years later, in 1806) and sent it off to her with the ducats, saying that as a professional composer he would rather have a pair of garters as a keepsake.

A pair of red-and-white knit garters duly arrived, along with a note saying that if Haydn didn't hear anything further from her, the plan had failed and she, ill with consumption, had departed this vale of tears.

The story ends there. Haydn heard no more from her and could only assume that the unfortunate lady had succumbed to a combination of consumption and a broken heart.

QUESTION
12

Match the Haydn work on the left with its nickname on the right.

Mass No. 9 in D Minor – A   1 – "London"

String Quartet in C, – B   2 – "Lord Nelson"
Op. 76 No. 3

Symphony No. 45 – c   3 – "Emperor"
in F Sharp Minor

Symphony No. 94 in G – D   4 – "Surprise"

Symphony No. 100 in G – E   5 – "Farewell"

Symphony No. 101 in D – F   6 – "Clock"

Symphony No. 103 – G   7 – "Military"
in E Flat

Symphony No. 104 in D – H   8 – "Drum Roll"

A Memory to Cherish Always

During the time of the Second World War, Sir Rudolf Bing, future manager of the Metropolitan Opera, and John Christie, founder of the Glyndebourne Festival, were out walking with Christie's dog, Bimperl, who was named after Mozart's pet. As they strolled, they happened upon a group of soldiers who were among the many

Bimperl & Co.
A chance encounter with Mr. Mozart, the composer

helping to safeguard England's southern coast. Christie cordially asked them if they knew where they were. All of them hailed from other parts of Britain and none of them had ever heard of Glyndebourne. Christie then pointed to his impressive manor house where the concerts were given and said that Mozart lived there. One of the tommies nodded agreeably, recognizing Mozart's name. Then Christie pointed to his pet and told them that Bimperl was Mozart's dog. After staring downward at the animal, the soldiers nodded respectfully, looked up at the authoritative-looking Bing and said politely, "It is a great honor to meet you, sir."

Arrange the following events concerning Mozart in chronological order from the earliest to the latest.

____ A. *The Magic Flute* receives its premiere in Vienna.

____ B. Mozart composes his three most popular violin concerti, No. 3 in G, K. 216, No. 4 in D, K. 218, and No. 5 in A, K. 219.

_____ C. *The Marriage of Figaro* is given its premiere in Vienna.

_____ D. The Requiem in D Minor is performed for the first time at the home of the person who commissioned it, Count Walsegg.

_____ E. *The Abduction from the Seraglio* receives its premiere in Vienna.

A Concert by Candlelight

What is it about him? Is it the wild-looking hair in his portraits,his music, his mysterious love life, his abortive fling at parenthood in his turbulent relationship with his nephew? Perhaps it's the awful irony of his deafness, that he, of all people, should be denied the ability to hear the many wonderful fruits of his hard labor, enjoyed by so many millions of people. Whatever it is, the name of Ludwig van Beethoven is probably the one most likely to crop up in every day conversation about classical music at the dinner table, on the job, during a campus bull session—at any time of day in almost any informal situation.

If it is his deafness that evokes such fascination, then it should be noted that Beethoven's hearing affliction wasn't quite as severe as is usually portrayed. There are reports of his enjoying intermittent hearing almost until the day of his death. That he led the orchestra himself in the premiere of his Ninth Symphony tells us that he felt there was a good chance that his auditory system would be in satisfactory working order at that time.

When we read of the colorful occurrences at some premieres where Beethoven was conductor or soloist or both, we wonder how many can be chalked up to his hearing disability and how many to his eccentricity. As a conductor, the great man resorted to all manner of choreographic movements, compared to which Leonard Bernstein of recent memory would look like the Great Pyramid of Cheops. For a softer passage, he would bend down—the softer, the lower. At a crescendo, he would rise progressively with the swelling of the music. At the transition point into a *forte* or *fortissimo*, he would actually leap into the air, often accompanying the movement with a shout of which he might not have been aware.

Beethoven was both conductor and soloist at the premiere of his Fourth Piano Concerto. In the opening movement, at the first orchestral *sforzando*, Beethoven stood up from the piano bench and, in keeping with his custom, swung his arms wide apart, thereby knocking candlesticks from the music rack and onto the keyboard.

32

The Conducting Style of L. van Beethoven
"Fortissimooooooooooohhh!"

When the audience laughed, the composer began the new work all over again. To prevent a recurrence, the manager ordered a couple of choirboys to stand on either side of the composer and hold the candlesticks. At the *sforzando*, Beethoven walloped the boy on the right so hard a smack in the mouth that he dropped the candlestick. The other, more alert, managed to duck in time. When the audience redoubled its laughter, the composer became so livid that on the first chord of his piano solo he broke a dozen strings.

That, to repeat, was the premiere of the Fourth Piano Concerto.

When it came time for the début of the Fifth, the famous *Emperor* Concerto, at the keyboard was not the composer but a different soloist.

Match the person with the role he played in the life of Beethoven.

A. Archduke Rudolph   E. Kreutzer

B. Czerny   F. Salieri

C. Diabelli   G. Schiller

D. Goethe   H. Waldstein

_____ 1 German poet and dramatist whose text Beethoven set to music in the last movement of his Ninth Symphony.

_____ 2 German novelist, playwright, scientist, and poet best known for *Faust* whose verse Beethoven often set to music. The composer's incidental music to *Egmont* was written for one of his dramas.

_____ 3 Italian composer who, thanks to a recent play and film, is today best known in connection with another musical giant. Beethoven took lessons in dramatic composition from him when he first came to Vienna, and in later years spoke more highly of him than of his other teachers, including Haydn.

_____ 4 Beethoven piano student who in turn became one of the most popular piano pedagogues of his day. The teacher of Liszt, he wrote many keyboard exercises at every conceivable level of difficulty, which were used by piano students everywhere for generations after his death.

_____ 5 Extremely witty and linguistically gifted Austrian nobleman who in 1792, when the premiere of Beethoven's First Symphony was a full eight years off, became the first person in recorded history to speak of him in the same breath as established masters Mozart and Haydn. He was the dedicatee of one of the composer's most remarkable piano sonatas, No. 21 in C, Op. 53.

_____ 6 Piano-playing Austrian nobleman and composer. A student and devoted friend of Beethoven's, he helped arrange for the composer to receive a yearly pension to keep him in Vienna when it was learned that he was offered the post of *kapellmeister* at Cassel. He was the dedicatee of several of Beethoven's best-known works, including the Trio No. 6 in B Flat, Op. 97.

_____ 7 German violinist and former musician to Napoleon. Despite their contrasting political convictions, he and Beethoven became friendly when the former settled in Vienna, where he taught violin when a broken arm ended his performing career. He is the dedicatee of the composer's most popular violin sonata, No. 9 in A, Op. 47.

_____ 8 Austrian music publisher and composer who furnished Beethoven with the theme for his Variations for Piano, Op. 120.

Me and My Big Mouth

As a young pianist, Franz Liszt enjoyed exploiting the tendency of many people to judge art works, including music, by their signature. He would play the same piece at three different times, crediting it to one of three different composers: Beethoven, Czerny, and himself. When the identity of the composer was given as himself, he received considerable encouragement and was told that the work really wasn't bad for one so young. When it was presented as Czerny's handiwork, the piece was ignored. But when the composer was said to be Beethoven, the work was overwhelmed by bravos from the entire audience.

At a concert during the 1836–37 season at the Paris Conservatory, Liszt participated as pianist in two trios, one by Beethoven, the other by one Johann Peter Pixis, whose music was known if not liked by many Parisians. Either accidentally or by design, the Pixis trio was performed when the Beethoven was to have been, and vice versa. The former was hailed as a brilliant work, but the latter was felt to be, in Liszt's words, "cold, mediocre, and tiresome," so much so that many in the crowd made an early exit, charging Pixis with impertinence for aspiring to be heard by an audience that had assembled to admire a masterpiece by the great Ludwig van Beethoven.

Two or three years later, the London music critic Henry F. Chorley began a musical tour of the continent that eventually brought him to the French capital. One day he found himself talking music with a group of local concert-goers, and in the course of the conversation Chorley made the mistake of saying something critical of the Paris Conservatory. As a rejoinder, Chorley was told that someone who hailed from a country that had failed to produce a national opera had no right to act superior. The rest of the conversation follows, with Chorley speaking first:

"Well," I said, at last, breaking out a little impatiently as my antagonists became more and more supercilious, "you can hardly charge upon England such an instance of false enthusiasm as was shown here on the occassion of one of Liszt's concerts."

"*O, par exemple!*"

"I mean," continued I, "when he chose to reverse his [program], and play a trio by Pixis in place of one by Beethoven; and the Pixis trio was applauded to the skies for the grandeur of its ideas, as so superb, so mystical—while the Beethoven trio was hardly listened to, and pronounced stale, mechanical and commonplace. Am I not correct in my anecdote?"

These last utterances, driven home so vehemently, were met with stony silence by Chorley's adversary and the others who had assembled to overhear the debate. The person with whom Chorley was arguing was the very same savant who, two or three years earlier, had been the loudest to praise the Pixis piece as one by the great Beethoven, and to dismiss the Beethoven as the work of the impertinent Pixis.

QUESTION
15a

Only one of the following works was actually written by the composer with whom it has long been associated. Which?

A. Purcell's "Trumpet Voluntary"

B. Boccherini's Minuet

C. Haydn's Serenade (the famous slow movement from his String Quartet in F, Op. 3, No. 5)

D. Haydn's Toy Symphony

QUESTION
15b

Since 1971, PBS's *Masterpiece Theatre* has been using an exuberant Baroque fanfare as its theme music. Which of the following statements about the piece is true?

A. It was written by J. S. Bach sometime between 1717 and 1723 as the fourth movement of his Orchestral Suite in D, which is dedicated to his patron, Cöthen's Prince Leopold of Anhalt.

B. It was written by Handel in 1713 for the official birthday ceremony for Queen Anne at Whitehall.

C. It was written by Jean-Joseph Mouret in 1729 for his first *Suite de symphonies* and performed later that year for King Louis XV.

D. It was written by Telemann in 1705 as the third movement, "March," of his Trumpet Concerto in D, which is dedicated to his patron, Count Erdmann II of Promnitz.

E. PBS commissioned it in 1970 from Aaron Copland, the composer of *Fanfare for the Common Man*, who wrote it in imitation of a Baroque fanfare.

Mortifying The Flesh

One of the oddest characters Liszt knew as a young man in Paris was the violinist, organist, and composer Chrétien Urhan.

Urhan was so devout a Catholic that he might easily have been compared to some early, flesh-mortifying father of the Church. He would take communion daily at noon mass and fast until 6 P.M. Then he would dine at the Café Anglais, where he would begin and

Urhan at the Paris Opera
"Get thee behind me, Satan"

end the meal by making the sign of the cross. Behind his back he was called "the man in the blue clothes" because of the light blue frock he always wore, that color chosen to honor the Virgin Mary. An accomplished violinist, he was the leader of the Paris Opéra orchestra, though it troubled him profoundly. Urhan believed that by watching the ballerinas disporting themselves he would be observing the Devil himself and committing a mortal sin. About this he consulted the monsignor, who told him that playing in the Opéra orchestra did not disqualify him from salvation. But Urhan decided to play it safe. He insisted that his contract include a clause that allowed him, the leader, to play with his back to the stage. In all the years he played at the Opéra, he never saw a single ballet.

At one point he felt called to a clerical life and gave up Paris for life in a Trappist monastery. The experiment failed in a week. Perhaps he missed the exciting French capital, or maybe he missed the wife of his writer friend Ernest Legouvé. Urhan often called on Madam Legouvé, but it was hardly a tempestuous romance. He would sit with her for about fifteen minutes without uttering a word and then leave, saying, "Goodbye, dear lady, I needed to see you!"

An Inauspicious Début

Richard Wagner's path to fame and fortune was anything but smooth. The first time an orchestral piece of his was to be performed in public, he was so young—seventeen—and little known that he had trouble convincing the doorman to admit him to the theater. The piece was an overture, and during rehearsals, the musicians begged the conductor, Heinrich Dorn, not to allow this insane piece to be loosed on a poor, unsuspecting audience. At the performance, a volley that the kettle drummer executed on the second beat of every fourth bar amused the listeners, so much so that Wagner cringed with its every approach. The amusement of the audience turned to puzzlement when, after a lengthy and convoluted passage, the musicians suddenly put down their instruments, their work done. Wagner had forgotten to cap the piece with a recognizable ending.

His tail between his legs, figuratively speaking, the embarrassed composer slunk away from the orchestra pit and headed for the exit, where he again had to face the doorman. The self-important guardian of the portals considered his time precious and was annoyed by having to listen to Wagner's overture. In retaliation, he cast a chilling frown in Wagner's direction, one that was to haunt the composer for many years. For a long time the future Wizard of

An Inauspicious Début
The future Wizard of Bayreuth goes back to the drawing board

Bayreuth and musical dictator lacked the courage to venture again into an orchestra pit.

Wagner's overture, of course, wasn't and isn't the only example of Western music to lack an ending.
    None of the following were completed by the composers who began them, if they were completed at all. Death intervened in every case but one, whose composer laid the work aside in favor of other projects long before passing away. Which case is that?

A. Bach's *Art of the Fugue*

B. Mozart's Requiem

C. Schubert's "Unfinished" Symphony

D. Mahler's Tenth Symphony

E. Puccini's *Turandot*

Wellington's Victory a Total Loss

In 1835 Richard Wagner was living in Magdeburg, where the twenty-two-year-old composer was building a reputation among local music lovers for his skillful direction of contemporary operas. According to the terms of his contract, he was entitled to arrange a benefit concert on his own behalf, which he did that year by recruiting one of the most celebrated singers of the day, Wilhelmine Schröder-Devrient.

The concert was to be held not in a regular concert hall but in a smallish hotel salon. Schröder-Devrient was scheduled to sing operatic excepts in the first half of the program, to be followed in the second half by Wagner's leading the orchestra in Beethoven's *Wellington's Victory*, a bombastic musical depiction of the decisive battle between the Allies and the French in which Napoleon was finally defeated.

After performing her half of the program, Schröder-Devrient seated herself in the front row to listen to Beethoven's music, along with the rest of the audience. Wagner brought down his baton, and the orchestra began its characterization of the frightful struggle. The sound reverberated thunderously off the walls and furnishings of the small room. The audience, deafened by the roar and sensing the onset of shell shock, began one by one to head toward the exit, leaving fewer and fewer to experience the conflict. Finally, even the loyal Schröder-Devrient had to depart, prompting a universal retreat by the few remaining stalwart souls. The orchestra, undaunted, continued its pursuit of Napoleon. Wellington won his victory, but Wagner lost his audience.

QUESTION
17a

List the four operas of Wagner's tetralogy, *Der Ring des Nibelungen*, in the order in which they are intended to be performed.

1. _____

2. _____

3. _____

4. _____

In which of the *Ring* operas can the following be found:

A. "Forest Murmurs"?

B. "Entrance of the Gods into Valhalla"?

C. "Siegfried's Rhine Journey"?

D. "Wotan's Farewell" and "Magic Fire Music"?

Resting on One's Löwenbräu

In October 1842, after years of study, struggle, frustration, grinding work, and defeat, Richard Wagner tasted his first important success as a composer, a colossal triumph with the five-act drama *Rienzi*. The poignancy of the situation was not lost on his wife, Minna, who anticipated victory after hearing reports from rehearsals. To prepare for it she gathered a cluster of laurel branches and lay them that evening on her conquering husband's bed, so that he could literally rest on his laurels. Unfortunately, her tribute was to go unrecognized. Wagner got home late that night after having had a few celebratory drinks with friends. Blotto-eyed, he threw himself into bed, and in the same condition he got out of it in the morning. He never noticed on what he had slept.

Wagner Resting on his Laurels
In the arms of more pheus than he could handle

Match the Wagner opera with the aria, number, or scene that was written for it.

The Flying Dutchman – A	1 – "The Prize Song"
Tannhäuser – B	2 – "The Flower Maidens' Scene"
Lohengrin – C	3 – "The Love-Death"
Tristan und Isolde – D	4 – "The Pilgrams' Chorus"
Die Meistersinger – E	5 – "Senta's Ballad"
Parsifal – F	6 – "Elsa's Dream"

Hearing Things

It was said of the conductor Hans van Bülow that he was so accustomed to correcting his musicians that on one occasion when he was about to begin a rehearsal of *Carmen*, he lifted his baton and cried out, "Too fast!"

Something similar happened in the career of Anton Bruckner. When he was a young man, Bruckner worked for a time as conductor of the Choral Association of the city of Linz. He always insisted on precise musicianship and clear diction, striving above all for truly ethereal *pianissimos*. Once when he was rehearsing a composition by Schumann, Bruckner kept repeating one of the *piano* passages again and again, each time insisting that the choir sounded as shrill and brash as a trumpet. The choristers, growing tired of their conductors criticisms, decided that the next time the passage came along, they would remain silent. When they arrived at the passage, the singers fell mute. Bruckner went on waving his arms, smiled triumphantly, and exclaimed, "Ah, now it is right."

His Master's Voice

Bruckner lived during the era in which the German music world was divided between the followers of Johannes Brahms and those of Richard Wagner. Bruckner was solidly in the Wagner camp. He had an innocent, childlike soul. He wanted recognition but, as with many artists, he lacked the drive to pursue it and sometimes felt unappreciated.

One day his students decided to play a trick on him.

The composer had a flabby pug dog named Mops, whom he would leave with his students whenever he went off to eat lunch. In the master's absence, the boys played Mops a motif by Wagner and then proceeded to slap him around and chase him menacingly. Next, they performed the opening of Bruckner's Te Deum as they fed him something delectable. After several rounds of this, they decided Mops was ready to make his début as a music critic.

"*Meister* Bruckner," they said to the composer one day, "we know that you are devoted to Wagner, but to our way of thinking he cannot compare to you. Why, even a dog would know that you are a greater composer than Wagner."

Bruckner blushed. Even to be mentioned in the same breath as the incomparable Wizard of Bayreuth embarrassed him. But that a dog could tell the difference between them aroused his curiosity.

The moment had arrived. They played the Wagnerian motif. The terrified Mops howled and sped from the room. Next they played the Bruckner Te Deum. In the distance canine toenails. The happy pug returned, wagging his tail and pawing on sleeves.

Bruckner was visibly moved. Ah, recognition at last.

Bruckner and his admirer
During a performance of the "Dog Biscuit" Te Deum

Perfectly Clear

After making a name for himself in Moscow as a double bass player, Serge Koussevitzky studied conducting in Berlin and then returned to the Russian capital to found his own orchestra. As the son-in-law of the head of the largest tea company in Russia, he had the funds to accomplish his goal. While picking his musicians, Koussevitzky expanded operations even further by starting his own music-publishing firm and, still not content, made plans to gain control of all the publishers in his native land. With rumors flying that he was even going to build his own auditorium, Russians began to shy away from his concerts, believing that he was attempting to monopolize the country's musical life.

To revive ticket sales, Koussevitzky, knowing that there was no such thing as bad publicity, decided to ignite the flames of musical controversy. Musical taste in Russia was then divided between conservative composers and those of a modern bent, each faction having its vocal partisans. Into the fray Koussevitzky planned to inject the mystical Alexander Scriabin, a third force whom, he hoped, both conservatives and moderns would attack, thereby bringing considerable publicity to Scriabin and himself. The conductor traveled to Lausanne, Switzerland, where the composer was living. The purposes of his visit were to find out what Scriabin was then working on, and to persuade the composer to allow Koussevitzky to perform the premieres of all his future works.

Koussevitzky knocked on the door of the composer's study, and Scriabin asked him to come in. After the usual exchange of pleasantries, the conductor seated himself in a comfortable armchair, leaned forward, and asked Scriabin to describe what, if anything, he was currently composing.

Koussevitzky knew that Scriabin was a mystic. Still, what the composer described must have surprised even him. If ever the worlds of flesh and spirit met, this was the time.

After clearing his throat, Scriabin declared that he was about to start working on a passion play. Though he called it *Mystery*, it was distinctly unlike anything devised by Sir Arthur Conan Doyle or Agatha Christie and subsequently dramatized on public television. His *Mystery*, Scriabin announced, would put an end to the world as it now existed.

The *Mystery* would include an Armageddon Day festival, said Scriabin, during which he would lead mankind to a temple on the shore of a lake somewhere in India. All of the arts were to figure in his *Mystery*, in which the material and the spiritual would fuse in an act of love resulting in a return to primeval chaos, followed by a "new breath of Brahma." The process would take only seven days, but they wouldn't be days as the world at present knew them. Mankind would live through millions of years each day, as time sped up with the onset of dematerialization.

To be polite, Koussevitzky the materialist occasionally nodded silently in agreement. But he was probably lost in a fog.

Because animals correspond to the activity of the masculine, Scriabin continued, while vegetation corresponds to the passivity of the feminine, some kind of polar act or act of love between the two might be possible. Both animals and vegetation are merely symbols, creations of the human soul. The former correspond to the caresses of men and women during lovemaking, with each kind of caress having its corresponding animal. Birds "correspond to the light caresses that have wings," while as for "the torturing kind of caresses—these are the wild beasts," Scriabin explained.

Animals, birds, and insects, therefore, just *had* to be present at the *Mystery*. "How wonderful it would be," he exclaimed, "to torture the world with millions of eagles and tigers, to peck at it with caresses and to burn it with the caresses of the wings of tiny, tiny moths and the bites of the snake! . . . As in my *Poem of Ecstasy*, on this last day of my *Mystery*, at this last dance, I will fragment myself into millions of tiny, tiny moths—not only I, but all of us. . . . Perhaps by the end of the *Mystery*, we will cease to be human but will become caresses, beasts, birds, moths . . .snakes. . ." And on and on Scriabin went, after Koussevitsky, delighted as he was mystified, persuaded him to agree to allow the Russian conductor to give the premieres of all his future works.

Pandit Scriabin Ushering Mankind into a Brave New World
And all Koussevitzky could think about was his stomach

Scriabin believed that when the *Mystery* concluded, the world as we know it would come to an end. Koussevitzky has less grandiose expectations. He figured that he, Scriabin, and their wives would go to a fancy restaurant somewhere and put away a hearty dinner.

QUESTION
19

Match the composer with the immediate cause of his death.

A. ____ Ernest Chausson

B. ____ Enrique Granados

C. ____ Alessandro Stradella

D. ____ Alexander Scriabin

E. ____ Anton von Webern

F. ____ Jeremiah Clarke

1. Murdered

2. Suicide

3. Drowned when ship bringing him to the United States was torpedoed by a U-boat.

4. Gangrene that developed as a result of an untreated abcess on his lip

5. Bicycle accident

6. Shot when mistaken for his son-in-law, a Nazi official

Cutting Down or Cutting Up?

One of André Kostelanetz's most vivid memories in his later years was a luncheon with Sergei Rachmaninoff, the last time he would ever see the eminent composer. Above all, Kostelanetz remembered Rachmaninoff opening his glittering, jewel-studded cigarette case and offering him a smoke. When it was opened, the conductor observed a row of the shortest cigarettes he had ever seen. Rachmaninoff's doctor, it seems, had told him to cut down on his cigarette smoking, and the composer had decided to take him literally.

Sincere Opinions

Around the turn of the century, an English singer named Michael Maybrick wrote under the name of Stephen Adams songs that enjoyed a passing vogue. Few knew that Maybrick and Adams were one and the same. While journeying to the concert hall one day accompanied by his friend the composer J. L. Molloy, Maybrick was

Rachmaninoff Addressing His Smoking Problem
One must follow doctor's orders to the letter

told, "You have a splendid voice, Maybrick; what a pity you waste it on these rubbishy songs of Stephen Adams!"

Publisher William Boosey, the source for the above story, tells about being visited by a well-known composer who brought with him a new song of his for which he had a high regard. With the composer was his son, a little boy about eight years old. When the composer had finished playing the song for Boosey, he turned to his son and asked, "You've heard that before, my little man, haven't you?" "Yes," came the answer, "and we're all sick of it!"

In the mid-1750s, when he was at the height of his fame and popularity, George Frideric Handel often took a relaxing stroll in London's Marylebone Gardens with his friend Dr. John Fountayne. On one occasion, the composer asked the good doctor to walk over to the chairs located next to the band to listen to the piece being played. As they were seating themselves, Handel told his friend that he wanted his opinion of the music. Dr. Fountayne listened and then told the composer that he thought it was very poor stuff, so bad in fact that they would do well to move to seats farther away from the band. "You are right, Mr. Fountayne," said Handel, "it *is* very poor stuff. I thought so myself when I had finished it."

Handel was, of course, one of the most remarkable figures in what today is referred to as "early music," which may be defined as music written before the symphony orchestra gained hegemony in musical life.

Match the musician below with the capsule summary of his or her role in early music revival.

A. Alfred Deller   E. Sigiswald Kuijken

B. Arnold Dolmetsch   F. Wanda Landowska

C. Christopher Hogwood   G. Gustav Leonhardt

D. Ralph Kirkpatrick   H. Felix Mendelssohn

_____ 1 Distinguished Polish harpsichordist whose vibrant, full-blooded interpretations secured a large public for many Baroque works and earned that instrument enthusiastic acceptance in the concert hall.

_____ 2 Massachusetts-born harpsichordist, clavichordist, pianist, and musicologist who recorded a formidable quantity of Baroque music and who wrote the standard biography of Domenico Scarlatti. Calling all of the Scarlattis in the city directory for Madrid, where the composer once lived, led to the rediscovery of several important manuscripts and a new catalog of all of Scarlatti's extant works.

_____ 3 English harpsichordist, musicologist, and conductor who in 1973 founded the Academy of Ancient Music, known for its many recordings of Baroque and Classical music in idiomatic readings on period instruments.

_____ 4 Contemporary Dutch harpsichordist and conductor best known for thoughtful interpretations of seventeenth-century keyboard composers Johann Jakob Froberger, Girolamo Frescobaldi, and Louis Couperin. Appeared as J. S. Bach in a 1967 German film about the composer's second wife, Anna Magdalena.

_____ 5 Belgian violinist and a member of a distinguished musical family dedicated to the performance of early music. The founder and leader of a Baroque orchestra called La Petite Bande (after Lully's aggregation), which has produced many of the most zestful, idiomatic, and highly praised performances of the music of that period.

_____ 6 English countertenor and vocal conductor who, in 1950, eponymously founded an ensemble devoted to the idiomatic performance of early music, especially that of England. The part of Oberon in Benjamin Britten's *Midsummer Night's Dream* was written for this singer who is credited with restoring a demand for the countertenor voice in the concert hall.

_____ 7 Eminent composer, pianist, and conductor whose performance of the "Saint Matthew" Passion in 1829 stimulated the wholesale rediscovery of J. S. Bach's vocal music.

_____ 8 French-born English instrument maker, writer on music, teacher, and tireless champion of early music responsible for the revival of an enormous quantity of Renaissance and Baroque music. An early music society founded in 1929 takes its name from this seminal figure.

Bodily Wasted

During the latter half of 1866, Georges Bizet was living in Le Vésinet, a small town in the country twelve miles from Paris, where he was at work on his opera *The Fair Maid of Perth*. There he was paying attention to a young woman named Céleste Vénard, who would later be described as a poor man's George Sand. The Paris-born Céleste, who became known as "Le Mogador," was by turns prostitute, dancer, and writer, eventually completing sixteen novels, twenty-six plays, seven opera libretti, twenty-nine songs and poems, and a book of memoirs. She lived at Le Vésinet with her mother, a crotchety woman of the slums who resented her daughter's charity, and who complained about all of Céleste's acquaintances, especially Georges, whose brash manners annoyed her. Every night after returning from Paris on the midnight train, the composer would pass Céleste's house and rap his cane or umbrella violently on the shutters and then continue onward, laughing. Chills of terror would run up the residents' spines; the women would scream and the dog would bark. The mother's room was located just above Céleste's. One night, Georges began rapping on the shutter after noticing that the light was still on in his sweetheart's room. He did not continue on his way as usual, having some news that he wanted to share with her. Céleste called down that she was undressing and that she would be down in a minute. No sooner did she withdraw from the window than she heard Georges yell that he had just been doused in a surprise shower. The weather that night

Bizet at Le Vésinet
A great composer's spirits are dampened

was beautiful, so Georges knew it wasn't rain that was falling. He also knew the contents of chamber pots. He shouted up to Céleste's mother that that was certainly a shameful way to treat an innocent passerby. She told him to get on his way. He did, poor fellow, arriving home emotionally exhausted and spiritually dampened.

Like a number of composers who wrote primarily for the theater, Bizet produced one or two popular intrumental pieces unconnected with any of his stage works.

Name one popular nontheatrical work written by each of the following composers:

A. Smetana _____

B. Weber _____

C. Wagner _____

D. Bizet _____

E. Gounod _____

Whatever Happened to Me, Anyway?

The American composer and pianist Louis Moreau Gottschalk was one of the great Romantic virtuosi of the nineteenth century. Handsome looks, natty attire, suave manners, and phenomenal technique brought him a success much like that of Liszt. After establishing his reputation in Europe, Gottschalk returned to the United States in 1853 and concertized extensively in America, the Caribbean, and Latin America during the remaining sixteen years of his life. At one point his travels brought him to Mexico City, where the landlord of the hotel where he was staying proved to be a fellow French-speaking American from New Orleans. The man told Gottschalk the story of his life, about his former restaurant on Lake Ponchartrain and a thousand other things. He then spoke about a chess player named Morphy, citing him as an example of a New Orleans–born talent who eventually amounted to something, unlike that . . . what was his name? . . . Louis Gottschalk. Gottschalk, the landlord said, promised many wonderful things as a child when his father sent him to Europe to become a great musician. But no one has heard a blessed thing about him since, the landlord said. What has happened to him? he asked.

Gottschalk told the man that Gottschalk was still working at music despite his failure to realize all of the expectations of his countrymen.

Who am I?

Over the years, a number of well-known opera singers have raised the eyebrows of the Argus-eyed intelligentsia by moon-lighting as pop performers. How I sympathize with those wearers of two hats, for I spent almost my entire professional life shuttling between two musical languages. I, too, would dwell in the emotional world of one of them for a spell, tire of it, and seek refreshment in the other—until tiring of that as well. But unlike the opera singers, I used two different names for each. The classical world knew me by my real name, the popular world by another. And so it went for almost forty years until my death in 1969.

But please, don't misunderstand me. I was not a singer. No, I was a composer—a highly trained one of impeccable credentials who put his considerable knowledge of his craft to work in fashioning a few of the most exquisite popular songs of all time, whose titles and tunes are very familiar to you.

When you couple all of the traveling I did with the five countries that at one time or another I called my home, you'd have to say that my birth and background were portentous. I was born, of highly mixed lineage, on October 10, 1903, in the railroad station of Pskov, Russia. My parents and grandparents, people of some means, were of Austrian, Georgian, Lithuanian, Russian, and Spanish stock. Mom and Dad envisioned a diplo-matic career for me, but when Dad died, I was able to persuade Mom to enroll me at Kiev Conservatory. There I studied with the distinguished Reinhold Glière, the teacher of Sergei Prokofiev, who, incidently, became a close friend and staunch supporter of mine. When the Russian Revolution broke out, my family and I fled first to Odessa and then, two years later, to Constantinople, where I remained active as a composer. It was then and there that I had one of the most fateful experiences of my life. While working in a musical capacity for the YMCA, I happened upon some sheet music of American popular songs, of which George Gershwin's "Swanee," written the year before, was one. So enthusiastic was I for Gershwin and this new American musical language that I decided I would try my hand at it, too. A year later, in 1921, I emigrated to the United States.

Those first difficult years in America saw me working at a number of ill-paying musical jobs, including conducting the orchestra of a strip joint. But there were encouraging moments, one of which was my meeting with the great Gershwin himself, to whom I had gained an introduction. When he looked over

Who Am I?
On the way up, he worked at only the classiest establishments

my initial attempts at the popular idiom, he felt they showed
promise and suggested that I take the anglicized form of my
name by which I am almost exclusively known today. Another
bright spot was the piano concerto I wrote for Arthur Rubinstein
in 1922, which was to open classical doors for me, so to speak.

Two years later I took my concerto with me to Paris, where I
showed it to Sergei Diaghilev, the ever-so-influential impresario
of the Ballet Russe. So impressed with my work was Diaghilev,
an amateur pianist himself, that he commissioned ballet music
for a production of his called *Zephyr et Flore*. *Zephyr et Flore* did
not duplicate any of the impresario's sensational prewar successes, but it was performed in Monte Carlo (in 1925), Paris, and
several other European capitals. Meanwhile, I made another
important contact in the person of the conductor and publisher
Serge Koussevitzky, who brought out my most important works
for orchestra, including my first two symphonies.

In 1925, when my classical prospects looked bright with the
début of *Zephyr et Flore*, I moved to London, where I snapped up
my first commission for a stage show. The show never got off

the ground, but six songs I fashioned for a Viennese operetta called *Yvonne* were interpolated into that score.

I was now on my way. Returning to the United States in 1929, I wrote background music for Paramount Pictures at its Astoria Studio for a spell and then resumed my career as a stage composer. Soon I scored my first hit, "I'm Only Human After All," which, with lyrics by Yip Harburg and Ira Gershwin, was one of two songs I contributed to an edition of *Garrick Gaieties* in 1930. Its location was typical of my output at the time, in that most of my songs, including my best ones, were written for revues and the like. "Autumn in New York," with lyrics by myself, I composed in 1934 for a production called *Thumbs Up*. Through the years, it and "April in Paris" have been the best-loved songs that glorify a specific place at a particular time of the year. Small wonder that the two of them are often linked in the public mind. I wrote "April in Paris," too.

With lyrics by Harburg, this evocative song débuted in 1932 in the first production for which I composed the entire score, a Beatrice Lillie vehicle called *Walk a Little Faster*. Miss Lillie and her colleagues may have walked fast, but my song didn't. "April in Paris" had to endure several years of being overlooked before its revival on the nightclub circuit and on a recording by a once well-known society chanteuse named Marian Chase.

In the mid-thirties, the *Ziegfeld Follies* kept me busy. For the *Follies* of 1934, I penned three hits, "What Is There to Say?" "I Like the Likes of You," and "Suddenly," and for the edition of the following year, I came up with a song that would become a basic item in the repertoire of many Swing Era ballad singers, "I Can't Get Started with You."

I was summoned to Hollywood in 1937 under circumstances that I wished had not transpired. Sam Goldwyn hired me to finish the score for *The Goldwyn Follies*, which my idol and friend George Gershwin had been working on at the time of his early death. My efforts were more remarkable for the versatility they displayed than anything else. For this film, I wrote the music for one song, lyrics for three of Gershwin's, and a considerable amount of ballet music.

By far, my most successful Broadway musical was the fantasy *Cabin in the Sky*, which opened on October 25, 1940, with an all-black cast headed by Ethel Waters. In later years, it would be remembered for the song "Taking a Chance on Love"—an impressive vehicle for Miss Waters—and George Balanchine's marvelous choreography. A rather stilted film version with the same star followed three years later.

During the Second World War, while serving in the Coast Guard, I wrote the music for a revue that starred a then-unknown comedian named Sid Caesar.

After the war, I continued my practice of wearing two musical hats. Wearing one hat, I wrote several Broadway musicals, of which none came close to duplicating the success of *Cabin in the Sky*, while wearing the other I composed several ballet scores at the behest of such prestigious patrons as the San Francisco Ballet and Roland Petit. Perhaps my most noteworthy accomplishments in the fifties and sixties were two zesty books: my autobiography, *Passport to Paris* (1955), and a stylishly amusing attack on modern concert music, *Listen Here: A Critical Essay on Music Depreciation* (1963). The latter contained a long polemic against Igor Stravinsky, in which, among other things, I called attention to some of the inaccuracies in his books.

I spent some of the remaining time left to me translating the lyrics of American popular songs into Russian for broadcast into the Soviet Union on Radio Liberty. Also keeping me busy in my last years was a musical based on the life of Mark Twain. I passed away of heart failure on January 16, 1969.

Who am I?

Drama within the Delian League

It was said of the Englishman Frederick Delius that he decided to become a composer after hearing black field hands singing on his orange plantation in Florida. The twenty-two-year-old Delius migrated to the Sunshine State in 1884 after his German-born father had tried to force him to enter the family wool business. His existence in Florida not only put him on the road he was to explore for the rest of his life, but also led to the cause of his death. It was probably while living there that he contracted the syphilitic infection from which he was to waste away over the next fifty years or so. After residing in Danville, Virginia, New York City, Leipzig (to study at the Conservatory), and Florida again, Delius settled in 1897 in Grez-sur-Loing, a French village some sixty-five kilometers from Paris. He was now living with his future wife, the painter Jelka Rosen, the two having been drawn together the year before by a mutual interest in the writings of the German philosopher Friedrich Nietzsche.

Blind and paralyzed by 1928, Delius received a fan letter from a young Yorkshire composer named Eric Fenby, which led to the latter's being invited to visit at Grez. For the next six years, until

Delius's death, Fenby neglected his own music to serve as Delius's amanuensis, writing down music, including complete orchestral scores, by dictation. For more reasons than one, the job wasn't easy. Even to Fenby, Delius was often a disagreeable companion, blunt-spoken to the point of being insulting. The composer's musical opinions seemed as whimsical and changeable as the views of his idol, Nietzsche. On at least one subject, however, Delius never wavered—modern music. He hated it, being particularly ill-disposed toward Stravinsky and other composers who, he felt, approached listeners with written explanations of their music instead of the music itself.

Many people attempted to cure Delius of his blindness. One summer, a Scotsman named Erskine came to Grez hoping to restore Delius's sight through the medium of hypnotism. Exactly what the treatment was that Erskine employed during his two-week stay no one knew, but on the second day, when the composer went on his walking exercise attended by his wife and nurse, he tottered three times as far as he normally did without tiring himself. The next day, instead of being carried to his chair in the living room as usual, he walked into the house with little assistance, completing the journey by ascending two steps into the living room. By the end of the first week, Delius was able to remove his handkerchief from his breast pocket, dab his brow with it, and touch his face with his index finger whenever Erskine told him to. Though the Scotsman admitted that Delius was the most difficult case he had ever encountered, he assured everyone that he would restore the composer's sight, even if it were for just a few minutes at a time. If he had six months, he said, he probably could bring it back permanently.

After the second week, Erskine visited Fenby in the music room and told him that he wanted Delius brought up. He wanted him to sit in a chair without arms and finger the keys, hoping that the composer would be able to play the piano again. To Fenby, it seemed madness, but considering everything that Erskine had achieved so far, he decided to keep his counsel.

Delius was carried upstairs and put into the chair. As he began to fall off it at once, Erskine had to hold him in place by gently securing him at the shoulders. By now a crowd of Delian friends and well-wishers had gathered.

"By the time I count to five," Erskine said softly, "you will be able to sit on this chair without my help, but when I take my arms away you will not be able to move forward or say your name! One, two, three, four, five . . ." Slowly the hypnotist ran his fingers along the back of Delius's head to his shoulders. When Erskine stepped back, alas, the aged composer, try as he would, could neither talk nor move.

"Now say your name," the Scotsman ordered. As though freed from bondage, the old man spoke his name several times and moved about in his chair, backward and forward.

The dramatic moment arrived, one that the group of people in attendance, those closest in the world to Frederick Delius, had been waiting for. Everyone held his breath. "Now play!" commanded Erskine.

Without assistance, Delius raised his hands onto the keys. At once he began slapping at the ivories, producing a veritable cacaphony of tonal gibberish. Delius turned his head in the direction of Fenby and said, "Eric, the New Music!"

Though he was not one of music's great melodists, Delius wrote a number of pieces whose titles begin with the words "a song of," such as *A Song of the High Hills* and *A Song of Summer*. Name the composer of each of the following:

QUESTION

23

A. _____ *The Song of the Earth*

B. _____ "The Song of the Flea"

C. _____ "The Song of the Rat"

D. _____ *The Song of the Nightingale*

E. _____ "The Song of the Golden Calf"

A Predictable Reaction

Prokofiev's *Scythian* Suite, fashioned from a rejected ballet he had written for the Ballet Russe, was scheduled to receive its premiere in Moscow inder Serge Koussevitzky's direction. Because of the First World War, however, many of Koussevitzky's musicians were suddenly drafted into the army, causing the concert to be postponed. The morning after the concert was to have taken place, a savage review of the piece appeared in the Moscow press. It was written by the prominent music critic Leonid Sabaneyev, who had been Prokofiev's nemesis. He had been hounding the young composer ever since his works were first heard around Russia's musical capitals. His favorite word to describe Prokofiev was "barbarous." Sabaneyev concluded his lengthy discussion of Prokofiev's new piece by observing that the composer conducted it with "barbarous enthusiasm."

For reviewing a concert that did not take place, Sabaneyev had to resign in disgrace. Prokofiev, who made sure that the entire incident was well publicized, remarked privately that it made no difference whether or not the concert had taken place. If it had, Sabaneyev would have written exactly the same thing.

QUESTION

24

Textbooks define *program music* as music that attempts to express some extramusical idea—for example, to paint a picture in tones or describe a person or event. In contrast to program music is *absolute* or *pure* music, which has no other reason for existence than to entertain the listener. Thus, Liszt's *Battle of the Huns* and Beethoven's *Pastoral* Symphony would be examples of program music, while Mozart's Symphony No. 40 in G Minor would not.

All but one of the following are products of similar inspirations. Which is the odd item?

A. Debussy's *Prelude to the Afternoon of a Faun*

B. Granados's *Goyescas*

C. Respighi's *Il trittico Boticelliano*

D. Poulenc's *L'embarquement pour Cythère*

E. Matinu's *Les fresques de Piero della Francesca*

F. Dello Joio's *Scenes from the Louvre*

G. Hovhaness's *Fantasy on Japanese Woodprints*

H. Schuller's *Seven Studies on Themes of Paul Klee*

Creating an Atmosphere of Objectivity

Composer George Antheil enlisted in the American flying corps during the final days of the First World War, intending to slay multitudes of Germans and capture the Kaiser single-handedly. Ironically, after the war he ended up living in the once-hated Berlin, attempting to instill a taste for his brand of dissonant modern music. Antheil had been reading about how Chicago gangsters were wearing guns under their arms, so he decided to strike his colors as an American and buy a .32 automatic and a tailor-made holster to accommodate it. In late 1922 or early 1923, he gave a concert at the

Antheil in Budapest
An attentive audience for modern music is established

Budapest Philharmonic, during which the audience listened to a little of the music. In fact, they rioted. At the return engagement several weeks later, the composer strode calmly to the proscenium, bowed politely, and spoke briefly, asking the attendants kindly to shut and lock the doors. He then reached under his left armpit in his most dramatic gangland style and produced a gun, laying it atop the piano in full view of the audience. Throughout the concert no one in the audience even dared to squirm.

Athletically Inclined

Antheil did not drink much alcohol, and with good reason. Once in Paris he woke up in a strange hotel room to find the ceiling revolving above him like a pinwheel. He knew neither where he was nor how he got there. Lying in bed beside him was an attractive female whom he did not recognize. Still drowsy, Antheil was about to go back to sleep when he noticed that a trunk near the bed seemed to be moving. The movement appeared to be coming from something inside the trunk.

Antheil and Friends
Even for Paris, an unusual ménage à trois

Curious, Antheil opened it. When the head of a huge snake popped out at him, he sprang back as the creature slithered out of the trunk and onto the floor. Panic-stricken, the composer, stark naked, bolted out the door, down the staircase, and into the street, where he was promptly arrested by the police.

An influential and smooth-talking friend freed Antheil from jail. About a year later, he again encountered the young woman, who was plainly hostile to him. The manager of the hotel, she said, would never have thrown her out if he hadn't found out about the python. That he did so was entirely Antheil's fault. *And*, she added, her husband was quite put out about Antheil's sleeping with her.

After the composer told her how sorry he was, she said that he couldn't do anything to make amends at present because she was involved in a six-day bicycle race. But on the seventh day . . .

Not one to waste an opportunity, Antheil dropped in on her on the day she suggested. The first thing he noticed as he entered her room was her bicycle. By a clever arrangement of ropes and pulleys she kept it suspended from the ceiling when it was not in use. It was the first thing she saw when she woke up and the last before turning out the light. Antheil felt that that was singularly appropriate, considering her firm tummy muscles, slender waist, and how much she enjoyed all forms of exercise.

Antheil lived in Paris when Parisian musical life was being spiced by a group of composers inspired by the aesthetics of Erik Satie called Les Six. Who were the half dozen composers that made up Les Six?

A. Berlioz, Bizet, Chabrier, Gounod, Massenet, Saint-Saens

B. Debussy, Fauré, Honegger, Ibert, Ravel, Roussel

C. Auric, Debussy, Fauré, Honegger, Ibert, Poulenc

D. Auric, Debussy, Durey, Ibert, Poulenc, Tailleferre

E. Auric, Durey, Honegger, Milhaud, Poulenc, Tailleferre

(*Clues:* One wrote the first jazz-influenced orchestral work, a ballet called *La creation du monde* (1923). A second composed many film scores, as well as the song "Where Is Your Heart?," the theme from the movie *Moulin Rouge*. A third, somewhat more musically conservative in his later years, wrote three pieces for wind instrument and piano that are solidly in the chamber music repertoire. A fourth, inspired by the movements of machines, wrote an orchestral work called *Pacific 231* descriptive of an American locomotive. A fifth was a woman and a sixth was a staunch Communist who, among other things, wrote several musical settings of the writings of Mao Tse-tung and Ho Chi Minh.)

Defective Apparatuses

At George Antheil's first Europen recital, in London's Wigmore Hall, he played a Chopin piece, a Mozart sonata, something by Schoenberg, and one or two compositions of his own. When the recital began, Antheil spotted an elderly lady in the first row holding an enormous ear trumpet to her head. The Chopin flowed into her ear trumpet and made her smile. Next came the Mozart sonata. It, too, entered her trumpet and made her smile. Then Antheil began playing the second half of the concert, pieces by Schoenberg and himself. During the Schoenberg, the lady looked puzzled and began to shake her ear trumpet. Then she held it up to her ear and listened attentively, only to find no improvement. Her smile turned into a look of distress. She gave it one more try. Still the same problem. With a shrug of her shoulders, she put the instrument into her handbag and left. Clearly it was time to talk to the nice repairman at the corner store who would fix her ear trumpet.

A Schoenberg and Antheil listener
It was the ear trumpet—no music could possibly sound like that

Rain Dance

If any further evidence of the mysterious power of music is needed, perhaps this incident involving Antheil will furnish it. When he and his wife Boski arrived in Hollywood in 1936, it began to rain. It rained and rained and rained, aggravating Antheil's bronchial condition to the point of distraction. Even during Indian summer, when southern California is usually dry and baking, the rain continued. And it kept raining through November, December, and January.

Antheil was working on a symphony that included a melody he had copied down at San Ildefonso, New Mexico. It was performed by the Indians there as they were finishing their annual rain dance. Boski concluded that Antheil's playing the theme on the piano every day was the cause of the rain. To him, the idea sounded ludicrous, but he kept an open mind and, at Boski's urging, refrained from playing the melody for one whole day.

It did not rain.

Immediately, considerations of the financial possibilities of this discovery came to Antheil's mind. He had visions of himself commanding millions, perhaps billions of dollars, going around the world turning desert areas into garden spots. But the wisdom of Boski, loyal and sensible spouse of the wild-eyed artist, prevailed in the end. She reminded Antheil that when it rained and rained and rained, his bronchitis acted up, making him cough and cough and cough. Boski took the manuscript and hid it in a place where her husband was never able to find it again.

Antheil was one of the most heavily publicized enfants terribles of the late 1920s and 1930s. Considerable notoriety resulted from the Paris and New York premieres of his *Ballet mécanique*, which was scored for, among other things, a siren, a player piano, two electric bells, and two airplane propellers.

QUESTION

26

The Greening of Death Valley
Antheil could have made millions

Match the twentieth-century composer at the left with the word, phrase, or work frequently associated with him.

John Cage – A	1 – Twelve-tone music
Paul Hindemith – B	2 – Forty-three-tone music
Harry Partch – C	3 – Third Stream Music
Steve Reich – D	4 – Neoclassicism
Arnold Schoenberg – E	5 – Gebrauchtsmusik
Gunther Schuller – F	6 – 4'33", a piece that calls for a pianist to be idle at the keyboard during the period of time indicated by the title
Igor Stravinsky – G	7 – Minimalism

The Woman Behind

Richard Strauss, while visiting at his uncle's villa near Munich, met a young singer named Pauline de Ahna. She had been making little progress studying with a mutual acquaintance, who had recommended her to Strauss. So steadily did she advance under her new and ardent teacher that soon she was being groomed for important operatic roles, including the lead in the twenty-three-year-old composer's first opera, *Guntram*.

During a final rehearsal, conductor Strauss stopped several times to assist the leading man with the interpretation of his role. Unsure of her own part, Pauline asked Strauss why he wasn't showing her the same attention. When Strauss explained that he was satisfied with her performance, she yelled that she wanted to be stopped, hurled the score at Strauss, and stormed off the stage. Because the rehearsal could not go on, the composer followed her to the dressing room, from which shrieks, insults, and imprecations could be heard. Then suddenly all was quiet. The musicians waited, wondering who had murdered whom.

Finally, one was elected to tell the composer that they were horrified by the shocking behavior of Fräulein de Ahna and that they had decided never again to perform in an opera in which she participated. When the representative knocked on the dressing room door, to his surprise it was opened by a beaming Richard Strauss, who announced that he and Fräulein de Ahna had just become engaged.

In 1899 Strauss premiered his tone poem *Ein Heldenleben* (*A Hero's Life*), which he admitted to modeling partly on himself. He saw nothing wrong with basing a hero on himself, inasmuch as he found his life as interesting as Napoleon's or Alexander the Great's.

This opinion does not appear to have been shared by his wife. The daughter of a socially prominent major general, Pauline Strauss could never shake the feeling that she had married beneath her station. Acquaintances of her husband were amazed to hear her say, "I could have been a great opera singer; instead, I chose to marry that musician." Her sneering reference left Strauss undismayed, and in fact, in his later years, he was heard to lament her decision to give up the operatic stage at such an early age.

Napoleon and Alexander probably did not have to abide by the house rules to which Pauline subjected Strauss. Whenever he entered the house—villa, actually—he had to remove his shoes to keep from tracking dirt on the carpet, even when in the company of important visitors. And whenever he had to interview an *artiste*, or woman singer, a screen would be set up in a corner of the room

Richard and Pauline Strauss
Did Josephine force Napoleon to take off his shoes?

behind which Pauline would sit to make sure that the conversation remained businesslike and formal. Only when the departing visitor was heading for the door would she emerge from her hiding place. Scholars of opera find it relatively easy to study the planning of Strauss's operas because his librettists shunned his home, preferring to communicate with Pauline's husband by letter or telegram.

Perhaps the crowning indignities stemmed from Pauline's opinions of Strauss's music. On the whole she found her husband's work, in the words of his biographer Norman Del Mar, "plebian, vulgar stuff, entirely derivative and undistinguished." One might have thought that she originated the witticism making the rounds at the turn of the century: "If it be Richard, then Wagner; if Strauss, then Johann." Her husband's opera *Die Frau ohne Schatten*, for example, infuriated her. After its premiere, as the two of them walked from the opera house to the hotel, she told him that it was the most dreadful rubbish he had ever written and that she was ashamed to be seen with him. She marched forward in a self-righteous huff, leaving Strauss to enter the hotel by himself.

And how did Strauss feel about her behavior? Whenever an embarrassing social situation forced him to say something about it, the self-styled hero said that it was good for him.

QUESTION
27

Match these female musicians with the capsule biographies below.

A. Eugenia Zukerman   E. Clara Wieck

B. Myra Hess   F. Mrs. H. H. A. Beach

C. Nadia Boulanger   G. Ethel Smyth

D. Sylvia Marlowe   H. Germaine Tailleferre

_____ 1   German-educated English composer (1858–1944) who wrote operas in three different languages to her own libretti, including one *Der Wald*, that was produced at the Met in 1903. Considered England's foremost woman composer, she was also a militant suffragette, in which role she wrote a rousing song entitled "The March of the Women." A number of lively autobiographical books and reminiscences also came from her pen, including several with eye-catching titles such as *Beecham and Pharaoh*.

_____ 2 Distinguished English pianist and recording artist (1890–1965) for whose determined concertizing during the grim days of the Second World War she was made a Dame of the British Empire by King George VI in 1941.

_____ 3 Massachusetts-born (1944) flutist, a leader in her field, who is also the classical music reporter for the popular Charles Kuralt–hosted TV program "CBS Sunday Morning."

_____ 4 Eminent American harpsichordist (1908–81), radio performer, and recording artist who in 1957 founded the Harpsichord Music Society, whose purpose is to commission new works for that instrument. Though primarily devoted to Baroque music, she championed contemporary popular music as well, even going so far as to perform in clubs with a group called the Chamber Music Society of Lower Basin Street.

_____ 5 World-class pianist (1819–96) whose efforts helped to gain acceptance for the piano music of the great nineteenth-century masters. She was the daughter of a remarkable pianist and even more remarkable teacher, the wife of a great composer, and the lifelong friend of Brahms. She was also a composer of some distinction, writing a piano concerto and many smaller works.

_____ 6 French composer (1892–1983) who was one of Les Six.

_____ 7 French organist, pedagogue, and conductor (1887–1979) who was the teacher of many of this century's best-known American composers, including Aaron Copland, Walter Piston, Roy Harris, and Virgil Thomson, as well as Europeans Jean Francaix and Lennox Berkeley. As a conductor, she was the first of her sex to lead the New York Philharmonic.

_____ 8 New Hampshire–born composer and pianist (1867–1944) who was the first American woman to write a significant body of work in the European tradition. In 1896 her *Gaelic* Symphony was performed by the Boston Symphony Orchestra; four years later she was the soloist with the same aggregation in the premiere of her piano concerto. She wrote primarily for solo piano, solo voice, and chorus.

Name That Tune

Being the spouse of an avante-garde composer can have its trying moments.

Oscar Levant was lunching with the Schoenbergs at their home in Brentwood when he heard the composer humming an inscrutable, atonal theme in his characteristic idiom. Schoenberg stared at his wife and asked her to identify the piece.

She hesitated, stuttered, coughed, hemmed, hawed, and finally admitted defeat.

Annoyed, the composer told her admonishingly that that was the main theme of the piece he had written for her birthday and dedicated to her.

East Meets West

Though the history of music has numerous accounts of famous composers who casually disdained or ignored the material rewards of success, many of them have secretly relished the adulation of the public. Berlioz, in his *Memoirs*, tells about a railway worker struck dumb upon realizing that the trunk he had just off-loaded belonged to the distinguished composer of the *Symphonie fantastique*, who was standing right there next to him. Berlioz portrayed the man as silly and the incident ridiculous; nevertheless, he included it in his autobiography for all the world to read.

Not every composer has been as fortunate as he. When Arnold Schoenberg settled in the Los Angeles area in the 1930s, he was befriended by—of all people—Oscar Levant, who acted as his social advisor and occasional chauffeur. Schoenberg's musical influence and Levant's remarks about the composer's fine character persuaded Harpo Marx to invite Schoenberg to a dinner at his house where he would be the guest of honor. By this time Schoenberg already was long famous for his scorn for popular culture and his I'll-not-sully-my-genius-by-writing-for-the-masses philosophy. And so, to establish a more rounded social mix—as though it weren't round enough already—Harpo invited a couple of friends who happened to be in town: Fanny Brice and Beatrice Lillie. Schoenberg hadn't the foggiest idea who they were, and to them he might as well have been the man in the moon. In an attempt at polite conversation, Fanny Brice asked the composer of *Pierrot Lunaire* and *Erwartung* what "hits" he had written. After dinner, she continued to press for an example of his keyboard skills, urging him on with "C'mon, professor, play us a tune."

Arnold Schoenberg and Fanny Brice
"Don't be modest, Professor. Tell Mama, what hits have you written?"

Name the composers of the following works:

A. _____ *Appalachian Spring*

B. _____ *The Bohemian Girl*

C. _____ *Concord* Sonata

D. _____ English Suites

E. _____ French Military March
(Marche militaire Française)

F. _____ *Grand Canyon* Suite

G. _____ Hungarian Rhapsodies

H. _____ *Italian* Symphony

I. _____ Persian March

J. _____ Rumanian Rhapsodies

K. _____ *Scottish* Symphony

L. _____ *Turkish* Concerto

3

Pianists

Vladimir the Vindictive

Early in this century, the piano was frequently described as a singing instrument. Few were better able to bring out this quality than the exceptionally talented but eccentric Vladimir de Pachmann, whose idiosyncracies at concerts included talking to the audience in the front row.

On one occasion, Pachmann was scheduled to perform Chopin's F Minor Concerto with the Boston Symphony Orchestra under its music director, Wilhelm Gericke. As an event, it was to be the stuff that dreams are made of, though few backstage would have expected it as the performance approached.

Pachmann said he was having a severe attack of nerves and demanded to play with the music in front of him, a situation that was unusual for a soloist of his experience and renown. He also insisted on having his secretary sit beside him to turn the pages.

Gericke began the performance, and the secretary turned and turned and turned. As he played, Pachmann leaned forward to study the notes with great intensity. Only at the conclusion was it discovered that he had put the score on the piano upside down. He had complained about nervousness and had asked for the music solely to rattle Gericke and make him think that the performance might come apart at any minute.

The conductor thought Pachmann's behavior abominable and displayed no trace of civility when the pianist stood up to acknowledge the applause. It was the custom for the soloist to bow first to the audience, then to the maestro, and finally to the orchestra. But Pachmann, sensing Gericke's displeasure, bowed three times, very profoundly, to the piano.

The Illicit Trade in Ivory

The turn-of-the-century American composer Reginald de Koven, of "O Promise Me" fame, once dragged a friend to a Paderewski recital.

After a Bach piece, de Koven asked, "Well, what do you think of that? Isn't it wonderful, masterly, sublime, that delivery of touch, that thundering fortissimo . . .?"

The stubborn friend asked, "Where's the rest of the show?"

"Why, there is no show!" replied the composer.

"Well, when are the singers coming?"

"It's Paderewski alone," said de Koven.

"Do you mean to say," said the friend, "that the whole entertainment is just this one man at the piano?"

"Why, yes," responded de Koven, "but it's Paderewski."

"Well," said the friend, looking around the house in amazement, "if this isn't the damnedest scheme for money-making I've ever seen!"

QUESTION 29 | **What nickname or title do we associate with the following familiar works for piano solo?**

A. _____ Beethoven's Sonata No. 8 in C Minor, Opus 13

B. _____ Beethoven's Sonata No. 14 in C Sharp Minor, Opus 27, No. 2

C. _____ Beethoven's Sonata No. 23 in F Minor, Opus 57

D. _____ Chopin's Sonata No. 2 in B Flat Minor, Opus 35

E. _____ Debussy's *Suite bergamasque*, third movement

Campaigning for Decency

When the flashy nineteenth-century virtuoso Henri Herz was on tour in America, a Philadelphia society hostess, a leader of the local temperance movement, invited him to give a private concert in her home. On the afternoon of the recital, he paid her a call to check on the condition of the piano. He was amazed to find slipcovers that bore a strong resemblance to bathing suits surrounding the instru-

Henri Herz and His Hostess
What the truly well-bred piano wore that year

ment's legs. When he asked his hostess about this, she lowered her eyes in embarrassment and declared, "I did it because it is not proper, even for a piano, to display its nude limbs."

Not a Leg to Stand On

The aforementioned may be the source for the witticism that Queen Victoria always felt better knowing that the legs of her piano were covered. Another ruler prescribed a much more severe remedy.

The virtuoso Leopold de Meyer once was summoned to the sultan's palace in Constantinople to give a recital, but when he arrived, no piano was to be found. De Meyer had one hauled out of the Austrian embassy and moved into the palace reception room. When the sultan appeared for the concert he was horrified by the sight of that grotesque object standing before him on those legs. Immediately, he ordered the legs sawed off. The remainder of the piano lay flat on the floor. De Meyer sat cross-legged on a mat and played the program to the best of his ability. He was a great success. So pleased was the sultan with the recital that he paid de Meyer five thousand dollars—the highest fee that that remarkable virtuoso had ever received.

Leopold de Meyer's Command Performance
A recital that no one could call pedestrian

Match the nineteenth- and early twentieth-century pianists on the left with the brief descriptions on the right.

A. ____ Teresa Carreño

B. ____ Ossip Gabrilowitsch

C. ____ Rafael Joseffy

D. ____ Ignaz Jan Paderewski

E. ____ Sigismond Thalberg

1. Mark Twain's son-in-law

2. Composer of a minuet that has remained popular with amateurs and with concert pianists as an encore piece. Briefly a head of state after the First World War

3. Editor of an authoritative edition of Chopin's works

4. Liszt's opponent in his famous piano "duel" of March 31, 1837

5. Opera singer and conductor who starred in *Les Huguenots* in Edinburgh in 1872

The Piano as a Percussion Instrument

In 1878, when James Mapleson's operatic troupe performed in New York, Steinway and Sons provided a piano to each of the artists for use in the theater and at home. Before they left New York, the singers sent a warmly complimentary letter to the company; in turn, Steinway offered to provide the same service throughout the remainder of their American tour. In Philadelphia however, complications arose. While the troupe was dining, movers for a rival piano manufacturer, Weber and Company, pushed the Steinways out of the artists' rooms into the hallways and replaced them with their own instruments. The incident escalated into a pitched battle between the men of the opposing firms. For weapons, the warring factions had unscrewed the pianos' legs. The burly Weber men routed the Steinway fellows, who beat a hasty retreat from the hotel.

The Rival Piano Makers
A Steinway, a Baldwin, or a Knabe—do not invite one into your home

QUESTION | **Which one of the following statements about the**
31 | **modern piano is true in all particulars or without qualification?**

A. It has eighty-eight keys and two pedals.

B. It has eighty-eight keys and three pedals.

C. Having eighty-eight keys and either two or three pedals—the better ones usually having three—it is considered a percussion instrument because sounds are produced when a key is struck or depressed.

D. Having eighty-eight keys and either two or three pedals—the better ones usually having three—it is considered a percussion instrument because sounds are produced when taut metal strings are struck by padded mallets called hammers.

E. Having eighty-eight keys and either two or three pedals—the better ones usually having two—it is considered a percussion instrument because sounds are produced when a key is struck or depressed.

Small World

Around the time that Artur Rubinstein began concertizing in the United States, Josef Hofmann startled the music world by running off to points unknown with a married lady from a distinguished South Carolina family, taking all of her children with him. The enraged husband vowed to bring them back.

Rubinstein was crossing the Atlantic when, to his everlasting delight, he learned that on board were two remarkable pianists, Raoul Pugno and Josef Lhévinne, the latter having recently made a sensational debut in New York. They invited Rubinstein to take meals with them at their table, and they became fast friends.

The second morning out, Rubinstein decided to fend off seasickness by taking a stroll about the promenade deck, where he noticed a man in a cape and beret there for the same reason. When the gentleman asked if he were Artur Rubinstein the pianist, he answered that he was and continued to walk. But the man was persistent. He asked Rubinstein for his opinion of Pugno. Rubinstein told him. He asked the pianist for his view of Lhévinne. Again Rubinstein obliged. Next he asked Rubinstein for his assessment of Paderewski. Rubinstein responded one more time. Finally, the man

sought Rubinstein's opinion of Josef Hofmann. That did it. Border-
ing on seasickness and losing his cool, Rubinstein exploded.

"Hofmann," he said, "must have been nuts to run off with that
horrid-looking woman and all of those kids."

Quietly, the man admitted that the pianist was right. He was the
woman's husband.

QUESTION

32

Which *one* of the following statements about Artur Rubinstein is false?

A. A composer in his youth, he wrote the popular Melody in F as
well as a seven-movement *Ocean* Symphony.

B. He had a close association with Spanish and Latin-American
composers; a number of the pieces by them that he played and
recorded were either written for or commissioned by him.

C. He disliked most modern music, especially that of the atonal
and twelve-tone schools.

D. Discouraged by his lack of progress as a pianist, he made an
abortive suicide attempt, as a result of which he discovered his
lifelong philosophy, namely, to love life unconditionally.

E. He is the father of the contemporary actor John Rubinstein.

Out of the Mouths of Babes

If ever there were a performing musician who knew how to ingrati-
ate himself with an audience, it was Liberace. With a ready smile,
relaxed and gentle manner, irrestible and often self-deprecating wit,
overarching concern to please, flamboyant clothing, and impressive pianistic technique, Lee (or Libby, as he was called in England)
conquered almost all before him. Much of the Western world sepa-
rated into those who adored him and those who said they didn't
like him but secretly did. The winsome gentleman from Milwaukee,
half Polish and half Italian, with candelabra and ducal wardrobe,
seemed like a cross between Old World charmer and boy next door.

His early days on the concert tour found him playing the Terrace
Room of the Statler Hotel in the city that calls itself the Hub of the
Universe. Boston, in those days as today, was an important theater
town, the last stop, frequently, for shows bound for Broadway. On
the boards when Liberace came to town was a revival of the Ben

Hecht–Charles MacArthur comedy *The Twentieth Century* with Gloria Swanson in the role of the harried movie star.

The Terrace Room was designed by an architect who knew little about the habits and whims of a showbiz audience. The only way someone could get in or out was to cross the dance floor, which was also the only space that provided enough room for the entertainers to perform. The touring musician learns to cope with any number of less-than-ideal conditions.

On the evening in question, Liberace, as usual, had the audience eating out of his well-manicured hands. In one of his engaging routines, he would pluck an absolute novice from the audience and coach him or her to play on cue a strategically placed chord or series of notes from a well-known classical piece. That night's "victim" was a precocious little girl who answered his questions about herself so loudly and forthrightly that it seemed to him she had expected to be chosen. When, after a brief exchange, he asked her, "Do you know who I am, honey?" she responded ingeniously, "Don't *you* know who you are?" and got a big laugh. Then Liberace proceeded to coach her in the musical routine, after which he thanked her and gave her several gifts for being a good sport.

A few minutes later, he was in the middle of an exceptionally poetic reading of "Clair de lune" when on his radar, so to speak, he picked up a couple of people tiptoeing across the dance floor. It was the little girl and her mother. "Where are you going, honey?" Liberace called out as he continued to play, knowing that the *Twentieth Century* crowd had already left.

She looked back over her shoulder and yelled back, "I'm going to take a piss."

Her mom yanked her out the door in a manner reminiscent of Margaret Hamilton pulling on Judy Garland in *The Wizard of Oz*. It was the last that Liberace and the audience saw of the little girl and her mother. Liberace picked up their check.

QUESTION
33

Liberace enjoyed coaching novices in duet playing. In a typical installment of his TV show in the fifties, his violinist brother, George, would play a dreamy ballad or two as Lee accompanied him at the keyboard.

Which *one* of the following pairs of musicians is not a professional piano duo?

A. Anthony and Joseph Paratore

B. Ferrante and Teicher

c. Arthur Gold and Robert Fizdale

D. Katia and Marielle Lébecque

E. William Bolcom and Joan Morris

We All Have Our Priorities

On opening night at the Adolphus Hotel in Dallas, Liberace spotted an enthusiastic and nattily caparisoned young man in the front row with a red rose in his lapel and a bucket of champagne beside him. The pianist couldn't have asked for a better audience. At the end of every number, the young man applauded as though it were the last and shouted, "Bravo, Liberace!" Soon, out of appreciation, Liberace found himself playing to the man, which in turn inspired the man to even greater heights of adulation. So receptive an audience was he that Liberace was asked afterward in all seriousness whether he had him on the payroll.

The next night, as fate would have it, there again in the front row was the young man of the resplendent haberdashery, complete with red rose and champagne bucket. His enthusiasm for the man from Milwaukee hadn't diminished a whit even though he was no longer hearing the show for the first time.

The engagement in Dallas at an end, Liberace and his entourage moved on to Miami Beach, where on opening night he came out and, to his amazement, spotted the young fanatic in the same place at ringside. With him, too, were the bucket of champagne and the red rose. The temptation to say something to him proved too great. Liberace made a brief detour as he headed for the piano and asked him, "How are things in Dallas?" After the show, the young man went backstage and had a brief chat with his idol, which ended in his saying to Liberace that he would see him again on the following evening.

Two days later, Liberace received a surprise invitation to a Lucullan banquet in his honor that was to be given at the Fontainbleau by his young admirer. The most exquisite delicacies from around the world were being flown in for the occasion to be prepared by the hotel's ablest chefs. All would then be eaten by Liberace, his admirer, and a select group of friends accompanied by the mellow sounds of a strolling group of string players. With his well-developed taste for gourmet food, Liberace could hardly wait for the dinner to take place.

But it was not to be. The night before it was to take place, Liberaces's manager walked into his dressing room and told him that the banquet was off—not just postponed but *O-F-F*. The young man would not be at Liberace's nor any other show that night because he had just been arrested by the FBI. He had absconded from a Dallas bank with $250,000 after engaging in what might be termed creative bookkeeping. The FBI gave him the obligatory opportunity to make a phone call and assumed that he would call a lawyer or a well-connected friend. Instead, he reached the operator and had a call put through to Liberace's room, where it was taken by the pianist's manager. The young man explained that he would not be at the show because he had another commitment.

The commitment was to last ten years at the government's expense.

Who Needs Etchings?

One of the hits of the 1964 World's Fair in New York City was a show by puppeteers Sid and Marty Krofft called *Les poupées de Paris*. The puppets were miniature likenesses of showbiz celebrities such as Mae West, Maurice Chevalier, and Liberace "speaking" lines that had been recorded by the stars themselves. A few years before the World's Fair engagement, *Les poupées de Paris* had a formal opening in Hollywood, attended by the celebrities who helped put it together. When the Kroffts suggested that Mae West and Liberace attend the opening together, the pianist arranged for Mae to pick him up in her chauffeur-driven limo and proceed to the theater, which happened to be near his home.

When Mae arrived, Liberace, thrilled at having this epitome of glamour visiting his abode of which he was so exceedingly proud, offered to show her around. She asked for a postponement and said that it would be a good idea to get to the theater as soon as possible to take advantage of the press corps and maximize publicity. During the trip, the pianist told the originator of "Come up and see me sometime" all about his home and its furnishings, including several unusual musical instruments. When they alighted from her limo, sure enough, camera materialized and flash bulbs began popping all over the place. Liberace felt like a king as he escorted his queen down the aisle to see the show, which they both loved.

Afterward, at a reception onstage, reporters clung to the magnetic Ms. West hoping to get a quotable line or two for the next edition. At last, the moment arrived. A journalist asked Mae what she was doing after the reception.

"I'm going over to Liberace's home to see his gold organ," she said in her unique manner. "I've seen every other kind, but I've never seen a gold one before."

Though few remember it, Liberace had a brief fling at a film career, costarring with Joanne Dru in 1955 in a romantic comedy, *Sincerely Yours*.
Match the pianist with the film in which he had a featured role.

Victor Borge – A	1 – *Anchors Aweigh*
José Iturbi – B	2 – *The Band Wagon*
Oscar Levant – C	3 – *Higher and Higher*
Liberace – D	4 – *The Loved One*
Ignaz Jan Paderewski – E	5 – *Moonlight Sonata*

Tales of Oscar Levant

No discussion of eccentric musicians would be complete without mentioning Oscar Levant. The concert pianist, composer, author, movie actor, wit, and colorful personality made considerable hay out of his mental problems. Oscar entitled one of his volumes of reminiscences *Memoirs of an Amnesiac*, a condition from which he suffered after receiving electric shock treatments. Once, while convalescing at home, he was engrossed in an English movie on TV that starred Sir Ralph Richardson. Oscar's wife, June, entered and asked him what he was watching. He told her that it was a fascinating film in which Sir Ralph Richardson portrayed an amnesiac, and that he, Oscar, was eager to find out how it ended. June told him that he had just seen that same movie last week.

When neither of them were yet household names, Oscar had a date with a beautiful chorine named Lucille Ball. A friend told him that she had recently gone out with a photographer on whom she pulled a gun when he made a pass at her. Oscar met Lucille at the door and told her that he would have to frisk her before taking her out.

Oscar and the film composer Bernard Herrmann once discussed approaches to conducting Beethoven's Fifth Symphony. The two were commenting on the many different ways they had heard the first four bars played when Herrmann asked Oscar how he would conduct the Fifth. Oscar told him that he would skip the first four bars.

In the film *An American in Paris*, he appeared in a memorable scene as pianist, conductor, and sole audience (of hundreds of Os-

Oscar Levant and Lucille Ball
A young man can't be too careful

cars) in a performance of Gershwin's Concerto in F. In keeping with
standard practice, the music was recorded before the scene was
shot. Oscar was well into the recording session when he noticed a
candy wrapper staring up at him from the floor, disrupting his usual
state of frenzied composure and tempting him to make a mistake.
The candy wrapper was a Butterfinger.

Years earlier, he and Greta Garbo had both been present at a
small get-together after a preview of *Anna Karenina*. Oscar had been
summoned to meet her after being described as a terrifically funny
young man who was already a legend. So intimidating was her combination of beauty and mystique that the best the poor fellow could
do was to stutter nervously that he was sorry, he didn't get the
name. Garbo turned to a friend and said that it would be best if
Oscar remained a legend.

Levant not only was a pianist but a composer as well. Among his works was a *1912 Overture*, which he described as an effort to portray a year in which little happened of significance.

Most of the great composers from 1750 to 1950 were, like Levant, accomplished pianists. In fact, many well-known orchestral works were originally written and published for the piano and then orchestrated at a later date, not necessarily by their composers.

All of the following were originally written for the piano but one. Which?

A. Weber's *Invitation to the Dance*

B. Liszt's Hungarian Rhapsody No. 2

C. Mussorgsky's *Night on Bald Mountain*

D. Ravel's *Mother Goose* Suite

E. Ravel's *Pavane for a Dead Princess*

Oscar Levant and Butterfinger
Why couldn't it have been Cracker Jack?

A Project is Tabled

Around 1960 André Previn woke up one morning and felt that he was in a rut. After years of film composing and arranging and a little moonlighting as a jazz pianist, the classically trained Previn wanted to try his hand—hand*s*, actually—as soloist on a classical record. When Schuyler Chapin, future Met manager and at that time vice-president of Columbia Records, heard of Previn's desire, he hit upon an idea. After finding out what repertoire Previn would be comfortable with, he suggested that Previn fly to Los Angeles for an interview with George Szell, who was then guest-conducting the Philharmonic. The idea was to have Previn, with Szell and his regular orchestra, the Cleveland, record Strauss's *Burleske* for Piano and Orchestra. The interview was arranged; Previn showed up at Szell's hotel at the appointed hour.

Szell had a well-deserved reputation as a severe taskmaster, an image the condition of his apartment confirmed. Previn found it to be so clean and orderly as to be almost menacing. Maestro Szell, wearing rimless glasses that reflected light in a manner reminiscent of Charles Laughton's monocle in *Witness for the Prosecution*, sat Previn down and grilled him about his musical background. At last

Previn and Szell
Why didn't he bring his favorite table?

Szell said, "Well, why don't you play the piece for me?" Previn looked around but could find no piano. "I do not have a piano here," Szell said, "but I know the piece forward and backward. I studied it with Strauss. So just sit down at that table and play on the table."

Amazed at the suggestion, Previn sat down at the table and, as requested, began thumping away on it. After the first twenty bars or so, Szell stopped him. "That's much too slow," he said.

"Well, Maestro," Previn returned, "it's because I'm not used to this table. When I play the piece on my table back home, I do it twice as fast."

Szell shot back, "Young man, I don't consider that funny," and declared that the interview was over.

Arrange the following tempo markings in order from slowest to fastest as they would be understood by the contemporary performer under most circumstances:

QUESTION
36a

Allegro   Prestissimo   Vivace   Adagio   Presto   Andante   Moderato

_____   _____   _____   _____   _____   _____   _____

Arrange the following dynamic markings in order from softest to loudest:

QUESTION
36b

f   *ff*   *mf*   *mp*   *p*   *pp*

_____   _____   _____   _____   _____   _____

How Does That Go, Again?

The distinguished German pianist Egon Petri once sat down in the concert hall to perform Beethoven's Fourth Piano Concerto only to find that he had forgotten the beginning. His problems, in fact, were twofold. First, he had forgotten that it was he, the soloist, and not the orchestra who had to play the opening bars of the piece. He nodded to the conductor to begin; the conductor nodded back. Petri responded with another nod of his own. And so it went for a few minutes, with each determined to have the last nod. Eventually, it dawned on the pianist that the first move was his. But his

85

memory drew a blank. How did those first four bars go? Petri got up, walked over to the conductor, took a nonchalant, over-the-shoulder look at the score, returned to the piano, and began.

Melody in F in C

Except for big-name conductors and soloists, are there any people making a lot of money from classical music these days? Not many. But there are a few: executives at some record companies and at some classical radio stations in big cities and top administrators of some symphony orchestras and opera companies. With the contemporary composer reaching new depths of unpopularity, however, publishers have to reissue and repackage older music to maintain their baronial estates in Westchester.

But is even this a pipe dream? Is it unrealistic to think that someone can make a fortune today from Beethoven, Chopin, and Brahms? Is there such a person nowadays?

Yes, there is—or at least *was*, if you care to go back a few years. Our eminently successful silk-purse-from-a-sow's-ear musical Midas was one Max Winkler of New York City. Max Winkler, whose career flourished about four decades ago, proved that the spirit of Mozart and the spirit of Mammon weren't all that irreconcilable.

Max's hugh success owed absolutely nothing to broad knowledge of classical music. In fact he had never set foot inside Carnegie Hall. As for the Met, it was merely a troubled place that he would occasionally read about while lazily glancing at the *Post* or the *Daily News*. To him, Florestan was a chemical that they put into toothpaste. Whenever someone suggested that he remain in the city for an evening to attend a concert or opera, he would resolutely point out that he hadn't missed the 5:47 to Lynbrook in *x* number of years and he didn't intend to spoil that record. As though to underscore his disdain for the music world, Max kept his office in Manhattan's garment district, far away from the concert halls. He wanted no part of them. If he had a motto that summarized his approach to the profession, it was one he expressed whenever he heard that some prestigious organization such as the Met or the Philadelphia Orchestra was embarking on a fundraising campaign for survival: "If they don't make money, why don't they close the joint?"

An immigrant from Rumania, Max at age nineteen landed a job with the house of Carl Fischer, slowly rising through the ranks and making the necessary contacts to establish his own publishing company. The house he co-founded and wrested sole control over, Belwin, Inc., did a lucrative business by selling to many of the day's major film studios, forging a virtual monopoly on the sales of musical cue sheets to be played to accompany silent films. This music, which sported evocative titles, took the form of simplifications, distortions, and imitations of well-known classical melodies.

In 1944 Max inaugurated Belwin's Educational Series, hiring as his arranger a Milwaukee schoolteacher named John W. Schaum. Max theorized that practically everyone in Christendom between the ages of four and ten is forced to take piano lessons by a parent, usually a mother. Being small and weak makes us defenseless, meaning that somewhere along the line, like it or not, Mom will plop us on a bench and bring us face to face with a horizontal row of eighty-eight black and white keys. Soon we will be big, rebellious, and stubborn, but by that time, Mom will have bought us a considerable amount of piano music. Someone has to supply Mom's demand. That was where Max came in.

To make sure that the music he published was within the ability of as many kids as possible, Max had it simplified down to the bare bones. One piece of which he was always especially fond was Rubinstein's "Melody in F." Good as it was, it could have been better. The trouble with "Melody in F" was that, being in F major, its key signature had one flat in it, putting it beyond the ability of many kid pianists, the ones who hadn't begun to learn about black keys. Max solved this crisis by having his arranger transpose the piece into the major key that is guiltless of any such foolishness as sharps or flats—C major. Thus "Melody in F" in C.

Music's distinctions, subtle or otherwise, were totally lost on Max. One of his all-time bestsellers was an edition of Debussy's *Afternoon of a Faun* whose cover showed a doe and a buck grazing in the company of their offspring, a fawn. When someone pointed out to Max that what the great Impressionist had in mind was an *f-a-u-n*, not an *f-a-w-n*, he grew annoyed. He replied that he had sold 350,000 copies of the piece at a profit of eight cents a copy when it had an *f-a-w-n* on the cover. That's twenty-eight grand off one lousy piece, and here's the Met and them who can't pull through without begging for dough!

Faun, schmaun. Shoot, what's the dif?

The Max Winkler Edition
Undoubtedly just what the composer had in mind

Are you "C" sharp? You will have the right answer when you answer "Cliburn" if you are ever asked for the name of the pianist on the first million-selling classical hi-fi record. But can you fill in the following blanks?

A. C_____ Exhibitionistic American avant-gardist, or place where batting practice is taken.

B. C_____ Elizabethan composer Thomas, or Allingham sleuth.

C. C_____ Transsexual electronics virtuoso Wendy, or international hit man "The Jackal."

D. C_____ American composer of *Skyscrapers*, or late lamented anorexic pop singer, or most hallowed tradesman in Christendom.

E. C_____ Berlioz's, Schumann's, and Thomson's other musical profession, or 1779 burlesque by Richard Brinsley Sheridan.

F. C_____ Boston composer George Whitefield, or fifties female English channel swimmer Florence.

G. C_____ *Louise* composer, whose surname sounds like Manassa Mauler adversary Georges.

H. C_____ Distinguished Mexican composer (1899–1978), or California farm workers' union chief.

I. C_____ Italian pianist Aldo, or Chico Marx role in *Duck Soup*.

J. C_____ Composer non Papa's first name, or Roger the Rocket's last one.

K. C_____ Polish piano poet, or writer Kate.

L. C_____ Long-feared Chicago music critic Claudia, or famous Bill Boyd film and TV role, or fifties Ohio State and Detroit Lion running back Howard.

M. C_____ First Met manager Heinrich, or late TV actor Hans.

N. C_____ American composer of *Ancient Voices of Children*, or particle of bread or cake.

O. C_____ The series of chords that signal the end of a musical phrase, period or composition, or the label the Chordettes recorded for.

P. C_____ Opera by Wolf, or Manila Bay island site of the Allied loss in May 1942 later retaken in March 1945.

Q. C_____ Verdi's model for Violetta, or Valencienne's wooer in *The Merry Widow*, or what comes before Saint-Saëns.

R. C_____ Offenbach's is the most famous one, or Cole Porter musical film that shocked Nikita in Hollywood (hyphenated).

S. C_____ The strictest form of melodic imitation, or how the Sherlockians refer to the Doubleday edition of the Holmes stories.

T. C_____ Rimsky-Korsakoff and Tchaikovsky each wrote a popular one, or another word for whim, or a 1967 comedy-mystery starring Doris Day and Richard Harris.

u. _C_____ Clifford, Ashley-Cooper, Buckingham, Arlington, and Lauderdale made up the first one, or what Rossini's *Barber* fell victim to at its premiere.

v. _C_____ Met tenor Richard (1900–1972), or what you hope your locks and security systems will keep out of your house.

w. _C_____ Bach's cantata BWV 211, or what is sure to wake up the masses.

x. _C_____ Paganini's Violin Concerto No. 2 in B Minor, or fifties Dodger catcher.

y. _C_____ Where Berlioz found his Eternal City inspiration, or a 1961 Broadway musical starring Anna Maria Alberghetti.

z. _C_____ Sullivan said it was lost; in the 1947 film *This Time for Keeps*, Jimmy Durante claimed to have found it.

4

Violinists and Other Virtuosi

Bull Sessions

The nineteenth-century Norwegian violinist with the odd-looking name of Ole Bull was famous for his staccato technique and for his ability to play four-part harmony on an almost flat bridge. In his performances, Bull frequently used a somewhat blatant showmanship calculated to appeal to the galleries. In America, his concerts often included "The Arkansas Traveler," one of the selections chosen to appeal strongly to locals. Whenever he played that piece, he would begin with a soft, melancholy section. At the end of it, he would lift his right foot in a manner reminiscent of old folk fiddlers beating time. Then he would bring it down with immense force and erupt into a frenzied, madcap reel.

Bull was giving a concert out west when a local farmer in the audience approached Bull's manager, Max Maretzek, and Maretzek's treasurer. The farmer recognized them as a couple of out-of-towners and asked if they were connected with the evening's program. When Maretzek told him that they were, the farmer asked, "Can't yer let a fellow know when all this confounded fiddling will come to an end?" He liked the music, but felt that "it has lasted quite long enough." When the treasurer laughed, the farmer, sensing an insult, said that he had a mind to whup him. The treasurer left, whereupon the farmer turned to Maretzek and said, "But, stranger! Why don't yer begin with the show? I would just like to see the bull, that's sartain, and then I'd go home."

Mood Music

Everyone has fallen asleep at a concert, or at least felt the urge to do so. Sir Yehudi Menuhin once yielded to the refreshing fingers of Morpheus during a performance of Beethoven's Violin Concerto *in which he was the soloist.* It happened when Menuhin was in the

Waiting for the Ole Bull
Dagnabbit, when will that gallderned fiddler git?

midst of a rigorous concert schedule, playing the Tchaikovsky in New York on Monday, the Brahms in Philadelphia on Wednesday, the Beethoven in Boston on Friday, and so on. With the Boston Symphony Orchestra and its distinguished-looking conductor Serge Koussevitzky behind him and a packed Symphony Hall before him, Menuhin dozed off, standing there like a flamingo during one of Beethoven's orchestral tuttis. Fortunately, the great man awoke about two bars before his next entrance, getting the violin to his chin just in the nick of time.

QUESTION

38

If the piano has the richest body of solo works, then the distinction of having the finest ensemble literature belongs to the violin. Better than anything else, the violin can serve as a symbol of more than two hundred years of Western concert life.

Which of the following statements about the modern concert violin is true?

A. Its four strings are tuned C, E, G, C, the second C being one octave higher than the first.

92

B. Its four strings are tuned G, D, A, E, each successive note being a fifth higher than the preceeding.

C. Its five strings are tuned A, E, B, F, C, each successive note being a fifth higher than the preceeding.

D. Its five strings are tuned C, E flat, F, A flat, C, the second C being an octave higher than the first.

E. Its five strings are tuned A, C, E, G, C, the second C being an octave and a minor third higher than the A.

A Nodding Acquaintance

Years ago, a soloist often did not rehearse with the orchestra before a performance, especially if the orchestra was one with which he or she had frequently performed the piece at hand. Fritz Kreisler, following custom, did not practice with the Boston Symphony Orchestra prior to a performance of the Beethoven Violin Concerto in the 1910s. However, it was not the Beethoven concerto that was

Sir Yehudi Menuhin on an Arduous Concert Tour
He shouldn't have had that glass of wine with dinner

scheduled to be played as he was anticipating. It was the Mendelssohn. The Beethoven begins with a long orchestral introduction; the Mendelssohn with a very short one, followed by the soloist's statement of the first theme. Anticipating a long rest before beginning his part, Kreisler nodded to the conductor to start and then relaxed his arms, holding his violin at his side. The conductor, puzzled, couldn't figure out why Kreisler didn't have his instrument beneath his chin. Kreisler, for his part, wondered why the conductor was taking so long to get things going. As in the case of Petri in the preceding chapter, a nodding match developed between Kreisler and the conductor. Finally, the conductor started. Kreisler almost threw his back out jerking his violin up to his neck. The audience had the violinist's quick reflexes to thank for his superb performance of the Mendelssohn concerto.

Go, Man, Go

Met soprano Grace Moore once went to Monte Carlo to hear Kreisler play. Kreisler was every inch the artist, with his ashen, leonine mane, his burning romanticism, and his rejection of flashy affectation. After the performance, Moore ran into Harriet Kreisler, the artist's humorous, bluntspoken American wife. Moore told Frau Kreisler that she wanted to go backstage to tell him that she had never heard him play so well. Frau Kreisler responded, "My dear, you are so right. When that sonofabitch wants to play, he can really play!"

Identity Crisis

In the greenroom of London's Saint James Hall, Kreisler was fielding questions from calf-eyed admirers. In swept an adoring dowager who shook hands with him vigorously and intoned, "I don't think you remember me."

Although Kreisler had never seen her before in his life, to avoid causing embarrassment he replied, "Of course I do, very distinctly."

"Oh, really?" she continued, pleased, "The time we met in Berlin?"

"Yes, indeed," said the violinist. "I remember it as though it happened yesterday."

As the conversation progressed, it became obvious that the socialite had only pretended to know Kreisler so that, unlike the other admirers, she could address him as an equal.

"Well," said the gushing lady in parting, "I must hurry along now. Goodbye, Mr. Busoni."

Name the violinist.

A. _____ San Francisco–raised violinist and Carnegie Hall preservationist who on February 23, 1991, without protection of any kind, performed a Bach sarabande for solo violin for an audience wearing gas masks during an Iraqi SCUD missile attack on Jerusalem.

B. _____ Also an accomplished pianist, this remarkable Russian-born virtuoso was physically assaulted in Israel in April 1953 after playing a concert that included the violin sonata by Richard Strauss.

C. _____ A charming composer, this violinist wrote two operettas and in 1935 announced that several of the eighteenth-century pieces that he had been playing as encores actually were written by himself.

D. _____ An exponent of yoga, oriental religions, and health food dieting, this San Francisco–raised violinist infuriated his Russian hosts at a UNESCO-organized music congress in 1971 when he read a speech in Russian in which he criticized Soviet human rights and immigration policies. On the Arts & Entertainment network, he hosted the series *The Music of Man*.

E. _____ Colorado-born virtuoso and 1974 Paganini Competition winner who, on September 12, 1974, played at a White House state dinner honoring the premier of Israel. In July 1989 he was arrested and jailed on Martha's Vineyard for cocaine and heroin possession, drug trafficking, and breaking and entering.

Sydney Salutes Special K

Kreisler's concert tour of Australia in 1925 began with a formal civic reception in Sydney. The acting mayor declared with flowery rhetoric that the Austrian-born musician was the greatest violinist alive. His was an artistry, said the official, that would live as long as there were sensitive hearts and minds. Then, at the speech's climactic conclusion, when the time came to pronounce Kreisler's name, the dignitary turned to an aide and said, "What's his name, anyway?"

QUESTION

40

As a composer, Kreisler is best known for a bouquet of charming encore pieces for violin.
   One of the following is not a composition by Kreisler. Which one?

A. *Caprice viennois*

B. *Liebesfreud*

C. *Liebesleid*

D. *Liebestraum*

E. *Tambourin chinois*

A Quiet Funeral

The future Broadway composer Meredith Willson and his wife, Rini, were visiting Willson's harpist friend Teddy Cella at Carnegie Hall, where he played with the New York Philharmonic. After the usual formalities, Cella told Willson that he had been troubled with insomnia for some time and that he was losing weight as a result. His explanation sounded like something out of "Alfred Hitchcock Presents."

Several months before, his telephone had rung at the highly uncivil hour of two A.M. "Mr. Cella?" asked a precisely measured, this-is-confidential male voice at the other end of the line. "Mr. Ronald Schmeen has requested a harp solo to be played Saturday at eleven at Pool Brothers' Mortuary. In connection with his funeral. Five hundred dollars."

"Plus transportation. I'll be there," said Cella, hanging up and going back to bed.

Friday morning at two A.M., Cella was again awakened from a

deep sleep by a ringing telephone. "He isn't dead yet," said the same voice in a low register. "We will call you."

Every morning at two A.M. for the next three weeks it was the same voice with the same message. "He isn't dead yet."

Then, on Monday of the fourth week, a different message came: "He's dead." Just those two words. "He's dead."

On the following day, Cella brought his instrument to the mortuary at eleven o'clock. When he walked in, he was surprised to notice that no one was there—no mourners, that is. No widow, no girlfriend, no children, no best friend, no business associates, no neighbors. Nor was there a minister or a service of any kind. The deceased had been placed in a rather large casket surrounded by urns, vases, plants, and bouquets of varying sizes and descriptions. Except for the funeral home attendants, the only person present was a smallish woman with an oversize hat who stood by the door and stuffed five hundred dollars plus expenses, into Cella's hands as he left. Then she disappeared.

For weeks after, the harpist had lost a considerable amount of sleep trying to figure out the strange experience he had just had. Who was the mysterious voice on the phone? Couldn't he have shown the old codger some respect by coming to the funeral?

A Quiet Funeral
The audience was in no position to be critical

"Maybe he did show up," Rini said. "Maybe the voice on the phone was the deceased himself." She added that the last voice, the one with the very brief message of "He's dead," may have been the woman with the money imitating the voice of the deceased.

The next morning, the Willsons found a note in their mailbox. It read: "Slept like a baby."

<table>
<tr><td>QUESTION
41</td><td>For each group of musicians listed below, name the instrument they play (or played).</td></tr>
</table>

A. _____ Woody Allen, Reginald Kell, Richard Stoltzman, Gervase de Peyer, Thea King

B. _____ Phyllis Diller, Dudley Moore, Alexander Slobodianik, Charles Osgood, Solomon

C. _____ Paul Zahn, Morey Amsterdam, Laurence Lesser, Jules Eskin, Paul Tortelier

D. _____ Carol Wincenc, Claude Monteux, James Galway, Paula Robison, Frederick the Great

E. _____ Efrem Zimbalist, Sr., Florian Zabach, Maud Powell, Erica Morini, Nadia Salerno-Sonnenberg

F. _____ Mitch Miller, Heinz Holliger, Pierre Longy, Harold Gomberg, Ralph Gomberg

G. _____ Susan Drake, Susan Jolles, Susan Miron, Susann McDonald, Susanna Mildonian

How Thoughtful

The story about harpist Cella playing to little more than a coffin brings to mind something that happened in the life of the distinguished nineteenth-century cellist David Popper. After Popper played at a funeral, a member of the family congratulated him on a wonderful solo and insisted the the cellist play at his funeral.

Popper replied, "Delighted, sir. What would you like to hear?"

None Dare Cry "Encore"

Charles Baudiot, a concert cellist in the first half of the nineteenth century, once appeared on a program in which, after an orchestral performance of a Haydn symphony, he came onstage to play one of his own arrangements for cello and piano. When he started the piece, the audience began to laugh. Unable to account for the reaction, Baudiot struggled to give his utmost in an effort to stifle the amusement. He failed. If anything, the laughter got even louder. When the music ended, tears of discouragement moistened his cheeks. "Why? What was the problem?" he asked backstage. He was told that what he had played was an arrangement of the very same Haydn symphony the audience had just heard.

For what instrument did all of the composers in each of the following groups write a concerto?

A. _____ Beethoven, Mendelssohn,
Tchaikovsky, Grieg, Rachmaninoff

B. _____ Beethoven, Mendelssohn,
Tchaikovsky, Bruch, Sibelius

C. _____ Boccherini, Haydn, Dvořák, Elgar,
Shostakovitch

D. _____ Haydn, Hummel, Molter, Torelli,
Telemann

E. _____ Rodrigo, Giuliani, Castelnuovo-
Tedesco, Villa-Lobos, Carulli

It's not what you say, it's how you say it

If anyone may be said to have had an affinity for a musical instrument, it was the great cellist Pablo Casals. At the age of eleven he heard the cello played by a group of strolling musicians and was captivated by the instrument. He enrolled at Barcelona's Escuela Municipal de Música, and less than three years later amazed the city with a solo concert. Casals then went to Madrid under the tutelage of the Count de Morphy, private secretary to the queen of Spain. The count conceded the teenager's skills as a cellist, but felt that he had a greater talent for composition. With considerable reluctance he allowed Pablo to leave Madrid for Brussels, where the boy brought a letter of introduction from Morphy to François Gevaert, director of the Brussels Conservatory. Gevaert advised that Casals would fare even better in Paris, where he could hear great music performed by no less than four orchestras, but asked him to stay a little longer so that the cello professor could hear him play. Casals consented.

The following day he attended class. "So," the cello professor said in a tone that mixed skepticism and condescension, "I gather you're the little Spaniard that the director spoke to me about."

Casals said that he was.

The professor asked him what compositions he knew how to play. The boy answered that there were many. The pedagogue mentioned one by name and asked whether he could play it. Casals answered that he could. The man asked about another piece—could he play that, too? Casals said yes, he knew how. Several more compositions were inquired about, and each time the Spanish boy said that he could play it.

"Well, now, isn't that remarkable!" exclaimed the professor in mock admiration. "It seems that our young Spaniard plays everything. He must be really quite amazing."

As laughter rang out, Casals felt his anger rising in response to the professor's ridicule. But he held his tongue.

"Perhaps," the man said, "you will honor us by playing the *Souvenir de Spa?*" This was a virtuoso item familiar to all of the students at the school.

Casals said that he'd be glad to.

"I'm sure we'll hear something astonishing from the young man who plays everything," said the professor. "But what will you use for an instrument?"

More laughter.

Casals was now so mad that he could have easily bolted, but felt that if the man really wanted to hear him play, he would play. He grabbed the nearest cello and began *Souvenir de Spa*. When he finished, one could have heard a pin drop.

The professor was awestruck. In a tone that mixed contrition, apology, and esteem, he asked Pablo to come to his office at once. As the two walked from the classroom together, the students sat immobile and silent.

Closing the door and seating himself behind the desk, the professor told Casals that he was blessed with a rare talent. He urged the boy to enroll at the conservatory and sign up for his class, after which he would see to it that he would be awarded the conservatory's first prize, even though that was not strictly according to regulations.

Casals controlled his anger as he told the professor that after having been ridiculed in front of the class, he could tolerate the place no longer.

Ashen-faced, the professor stood up to open the door. Casals went to Paris.

QUESTION

43

The cello is a solo instrument in all but one of the following works. Which one?

A. Mozart's Sinfonia Concertante in E Flat, K. 364

B. Bruch's *Kol Nidrei*

C. Brahms's Double Concerto

D. Strauss's *Don Quixote*

E. Bloch's *Schelomo*

Getting One's Money's Worth

After fleeing the Soviet Union in 1921, Gregor Piatigorsky settled in Poland, where he secured a job with the Warsaw Philharmonic. There Piatigorsky played alongside a fellow cellist named Slevak, an elderly gentleman who was something of a creature of habit. Long before the start of every concert, there would be Slevak, preparing his instrument and his music, lighting his pipe, glancing at the newspaper, and sprucing himself up.

One evening Piatigorsky arrived before Slevak did. He brought with him a role of fine but very strong cord and sat back to await his opportunity. Slevak arrived when he usually did and soon left the stage, whereupon Piatigorsky swung into action. He wound the cord several times around the scroll of the cello, threw the roll high over a beam above the stage, and tossed it to a stagehand confederate standing in the wings.

When the concert began, Piatigorsky was beginning to have second thoughts about his intended prank. He probably wouldn't have gone through with it if the guest conductor hadn't been an insufferably pompous exhibitionist. Piatigorsky gave the go-ahead sign to his confederate, who began to pull the cord. Slevak found his hands rising as he played his instrument. Slowly but surely it went out of his reach. Inaware of the cord, the old cellist stared in disbelief as the instrument dangled in midair. When the cello reached the ceiling, a burst of laughter dispersed the solemnity.

A Cello Soars to New Heights
A warning to cellists who are creatures of habit

Piatigorsky wound up paying two fines, his and that of his accomplice. But he felt that he had gotten his money's worth.

All of the following works contain a famous solo passage. Which has a well-known solo section for cello?

A. Suppe's *Morning, Noon and Night in Vienna* Overture

B. Tchaikovsky's Symphony No. 5, second movement

C. The "Dance of the Sugar Plum Fairy" from Tchaikovsky's *The Nutcracker*

D. Debussy's *Prelude to the Afternoon of a Faun*

E. Mahler's Symphony No. 4, last movement

Clarinets, saxophones, oboes, English horns, bassoons, and contrabassoons form the woodwind or reed section of the modern orchestra and are divided into single reeds and double reeds.

Which *one* of the following statements about reed intruments is true?

A. All are single reeds except the contrabassoon, which needs two reeds because of its large size.

B. All are single reeds except the saxophone, which is of relatively modern invention.

C. All are single reeds except the English horn, a member of the oboe family, which needs two reeds to produce its warm tones and graceful phrases.

D. Clarinets and saxophones are single-reed instruments; oboes, English horns, bassoons, and contrabassoons are double reeds.

E. Oboes, English horns, bassoons, and contrabassoons are single-reed intruments; clarinets and saxophones are double reeds.

Cello and Fellow

Like most people, Piatigorsky loved to travel, but as a cellist who was protective toward his instrument, he found it difficult to take it with him onto airplanes. To do so called for considerable cunning and stealth. He would conceal the cello in a telephone booth, and then, to while away the time, surprise friends with phone calls. When the departure was announced, he would casually pass through the boarding gate carrying the cello beneath his arm as though it were a towel or a newspaper. If the gate attendant looked suspicious, Piatigorsky would speak Pig Latin or smile dementedly to make him think that questioning the situation would be more trouble than it was worth.

Arranging a flight from Chicago to Dallas, the cellist was told by Braniff Airways that he could bring his instrument with him into the cabin. There would be no problem, they said, and they would feel honored to have so distinguished a musician on board.

Cheerfully, Piatigorsky stepped up to the ticket counter at O'Hare. Now, finally, the awkward, time-consuming game playing was unnecessary. With his cello on full display, he was a citizen and patron who had his rights.

Piatigorsky asked for his reservation. The employee joyfully repeated his long, Russian-sounding name as though he were expecting his arrival. While waiting for the clerk to apply the finishing touches to the ticket, the cellist looked about himself with the air of one who has life in the palm of his hand. Moments later, the clerk handed him not one ticket but two, one for Gregor Piatigorsky and one for Miss Cello Piatigorsky—$47.50 each. Startled and speechless, Piatigorsky paid for both.

Letting Down One's Hair

When Gregor Piatigorsky was a young man, he and the renowned conductor Wilhelm Furtwängler, both unable to dance, decided to sign up for dancing lessons under assumed names. Their teacher made a strong effort, but finally, in despair, explained that they were both unusually unmusical and should transfer to the section for slow learners. They decided instead to give it up completely.

Some years later, after playing his first Carnegie Hall concert,

Grisha "Finding Himself" in Harlem
If only Furtwängler could've seen it

Piatigorsky returned to his hotel and was told by the clerk that he really should visit Harlem. He described New York's black section as a place of great musical excitement. So Piatigorsky bade good-bye to his cello, hailed a cab, and headed uptown. In Harlem the Russian émigré found himself in a strange and exotic new world. Enticed by the sound of jazz floating from a cellar bar, he walked in and looked the place over. There he encountered woodwind intruments he had never seen before, frenzied exchanges between trumpet and double bass urging each other on, delirious cries from the dance floor, and waiters who unhesitatingly abandoned their trays to take part in the provocative dancing. Suddenly without warning the cellist found himself irresistibly drawn into the passionate atmosphere. He moved to the dance floor, kicked his feet, and shook his body in the most bizarre gyrations. Visions of having done so before in a glade in some primordial past ran before his eyes. A stranger to himself, he danced and danced until finally he found himself once more outside on the street alone. He breathed deeply of the night air and said, "Ah, if only Furtwängler could have seen this."

Match these black classical musicians with the capsule biographies below.

A. Samuel Coleridge-Taylor

B. Dean Dixon

C. Natalie Hinderas

D. Ulysses Kay

E. Wynton Marsalis

F. Phillippa Duke Schuyler

G. William Grant Still

H. André Watts

_____ 1 The most often played black composer, he was born in Tucson, Arizona. His output, quite varied and well within the European tradition, includes chamber, vocal, and orchestral music as well as opera. The nephew of jazzman King Oliver, he has penned an opera called *Jubilee* based on Margaret Walker's novel, and one entitled *The Boor* based on Chekhov.

_____ 2 This Mississippi-born composer (1895–1978) and one-time arranger for W. C. Handy became the first black to have a symphony performed by a major orchestra when the Rochester Philharmonic played his *Afro-American Symphony* in 1931. Similarly, his *Troubled Island* (1938) was the first opera by a black composer mounted by a major company (the New York City Opera in 1949).

___ 3 This British composer (1875–1912) was the son of an English mother and a doctor born in Sierra Leone. An admirer of Dvořák, he was and is best known for his three-part cantata *The Song of Hiawatha*, a desire to perform which led to the first of his three concert tours in the United States. A conductor of no mean ability, he was called by New York orchestral players in 1910 the "black Mahler."

___ 4 This Harlem-born violinist and Juilliard graduate (1911–76) was the first black to conduct major orchestras around the world and to leave behind a sizeable body of classical orchestral recordings. After guest stints with the NBC, New York Philharmonic, Philadelphia, and Boston symphonies, he moved abroad, where eventually he became music director of the Göteborg (Sweden) Symphony (1953–60), the Hessian Radio Orchestra of Frankfurt (1961–74), and the Sydney Symphony (1964–67).

___ 5 This world-class pianist was born in 1946 in a U.S. Army camp to a Hungarian mother and a black American father. At fourteen, he played Franck's Symphonic Variations with the Philadelphia Orchestra and followed it two years later with Liszt's First Piano Concerto under Bernstein on a televised Young People's Concert, creating a sensation. Since then, he has assayed many of the better-known works for the instrument, specializing in the Romantic repertoire.

___ 6 Precocious New York City-born pianist composer (1931-67) who at the age of fourteen appeared as soloist with the New York Philharmonic in Saint-Saëns's Second Piano Concerto. She traveled all over the world under the auspices of the State Department giving command performances for many heads of state. A co-founder of the Amerasian Foundation, she was killed in a helicopter crash in Vietnam attempting to evacuate Roman Catholic schoolchildren to Da Nang. She wrote five books about her life and travels. Mayor Fiorello La Guardia declared June 19, 1940 her day at the New York World's Fair in honor of her musical and literary precocity.

___ 7 Ohio-born pianist (1927-87) who was admitted to the Oberlin School of Music at the age of eight. She made her Town Hall début in 1954 and in 1972 she played Ginastera's Piano Concerto with the New York Philharmonic. Her concert programs included pieces by black composers as well as the standard repertoire.

_____ 8   This remarkable trumpeter was born in New Orleans in 1961 into a cultured musical family. The son of a jazz teacher, in 1984 he achieved the unprecedented feat of winning Grammy awards in both the jazz and classical categories.

5

Gilbert and Sullivan
and Other Theater Composers

The Great Arthur S.

Sir Arthur Sullivan sailed for New York in June 1885 to produce his and Sir William Schwenck Gilbert's recently premiered *Mikado* and to bring suit against an American producer who had been mounting an unauthorized version. From New York, Sullivan went on to Los Angeles to attend to a family matter, after which he slowly made his way back east. He saw as much of the country as possible, listened to its music, and talked to its people. One day his travels brought him to a rough-and-tumble mining camp in California, where he and his companions were to prepare for the next leg of the journey. As they pulled into camp, the driver told Sir Arthur that his arrival had been eagerly anticipated. When Sullivan disembarked, one of the miners who had been chatting outside a liquor store walked over to a muscular-looking chap standing next to the composer and asked him if he were Mr. Sullivan. The man told him that he was not and pointed to the composer. The miner looked at Sullivan with scornful disbelief and, after a long pause, asked him how much he weighed. Sir Arthur thought this a rather unusual way of measuring the merits of a composer, but went along with it and told him that he tipped the scales at 162. The miner seemed to find this odd.

The other man asked the composer for his name, and Sir Arthur said "Sullivan." The man next inquired if he were John L. Sullivan, the current heavyweight boxing champion. The composer answered that he was *Arthur* Sullivan, the composer.

"Are you the man," asked the local, "as put *Pinafore* together?" When the composer acknowledged that he was, the man told him that he was just as glad to see him as John L. Sullivan, and added joyfully that he would be pleased to buy him a drink.

Sir Arthur Sullivan and Friend
A couple of tough hombres meet face-to-face

A Grave Misunderstanding

Shortly after scoring his first successes in the London concert hall, Sir Arthur Sullivan was hired by a theater in Manchester to compose incidental music for a play to be performed at Christmas. In order to read a script of the drama, Sir Arthur traveled to Manchester, where he arrived in a light rain at the theater. There he was told by an employee that the script was still in the hands of the author, a skilled amateur who earned his living as the lodgekeeper of a local cemetery.

To find the author, Sir Arthur hailed a cab and told the driver where he wanted to go. They rode for miles in search of the graveyard; by then the rains were torrential. Sir Arthur may have felt he was in search of Dracula's castle. Finally, late at night, they found the lodge house, which seemed to be the only building for miles around. No light shone from the windows, and every inhabitant seemed to be asleep. After a long period of knocking and waiting, an old man with a nightcap and candle came to the door, cursed the visitor with short but vivid phrases, then walked down the staircase and unlatched the door.

110

The composer, his own mood eroded by the rain and the lateness of the hour, stepped inside. Across a flickering candle, he explained that he had just made a day trip from London to find out something about the plot of a Christmas piece. The old man listened in a rapidly rising state of astonishment, firmly convinced that he had just been roused from his slumbers by a lunatic. Had this intruder ridden in the rain in the middle of the night to ask about a grave, a burial plot, or what? Sir Arthur tried in vain to establish that he had come to talk about the plot of a *play*. The two seemed to talk to each other in a language neither understood, after which the composer, defeated, went back to the waiting carriage for the interminable ride back to Manchester.

The following morning, he found out that the driver had taken him to the wrong cemetery.

Match the Gilbert and Sullivan character with the show from which he or she comes:

Little Buttercup – A	1 – *Iolanthe*
Pooh-Bah – B	2 – *Ruddigore*
The Fairy Queen – C	3 – *Patience*
Mad Margaret – D	4 – *The Mikado*
Archibald Grosvenor – E	5 – *H. M. S. Pinafore*

Honest Self-Criticism

Sullivan once stopped over at a small town in the American West where his fame had brought him an invitation to a ball. It was a drowsy affair. The guests couldn't dance and the music was badly performed. The composer retired to a corner to nurse his boredom when a fellow sufferer came alongside and offered him a smoke. As he accepted the cigar, Sullivan asked if smoking were allowed. The other assured him that it was and then inquired if he found the proceedings as lifeless as he did. Sullivan said he did and suggested they escape. The other man said that he would like to but could not. He was the host.

Match each Gilbert and Sullivan operetta with its description.

A. *The Gondoliers* F. *The Pirates of Penzance*

B. *H. M. S. Pinafore* G. *Princess Ida*

C. *Iolanthe* H. *Ruddigore*

D. *The Mikado* I. *Trial by Jury*

E. *Patience* J. *Yeomen of the Guard*

_____ 1 What happens when a party of peers meets a passel of peris.

_____ 2 This colorful G & S opus, the last of their successful collaborations, includes a Spanish duke who, during military skirmishes, made it a point to lead his regiment while at its rear.

_____ 3 The only work of theirs in three acts, this attack on formal education for women includes a monarch whose day is made whenever he has something to complain about.

_____ 4 Inspired by England's Aesthetic movement, this features a pair of fancy-pants poets partially modeled on Oscar Wilde and Algernon Swinburne.

_____ 5 This one-acter was the duo's second collaboration and first big hit. "And a good job, too!" is an oft-heard refrain therein.

_____ 6 Flavored by music of a folkish nature, this includes a gallery of portraits that magically spring to life.

_____ 7 The most lucrative musico-theatrical property of all time, this features a good-natured executioner, an heir to the throne posing as a second trombonist, and a father who insists that punishment fit the crime.

_____ 8 Opening with an aria instead of the usual chorus, this is the only G & S operetta to have an unhappy ending. The duet "I Have a Song to Sing-O" is one of its most popular numbers.

_____ 9 This features a bunch of energetic policemen, some effective coloratura writing for the heroine, and the melody to which the words "Hail, Hail, the Gang's All Here" were later fitted.

The pair's first two-act triumph, this depicts the plight of a young woman who must choose between a wealthy government official and a handsome but poverty-stricken bloke in her father's employ.

Time Warp

Several places can be found in Gilbert and Sullivan where the spoken dialogue of one operetta resembles that of another. D'Oyly Carte tenor James Hay allowed his mind to wander one evening and, without realizing it, slid into the wrong operetta. The other character followed the wrong cue and suddenly the two of them were performing a different work. The act was almost over when Hay realized the mistake, stopped in midsentence, announced the error, and began the scene all over again.

At a Loss for Words

Sir Henry Lytton, who for many years was the great comic lead of the D'Oyly Carte Opera Company, began his career with one of D'Oyly Carte's road companies. After two years, he and his colleagues were released to find work wherever they could. Lytton got a job in a small town at a theater whose repertoire consisted of a minor drama, an even more minor comedy, and an operetta called *Tom Tug the Waterman*. Plays in those days were often put on by "winging it." One copy only of the text was kept backstage. Each player would glance at it from time to time to get some idea of the plot and dialogue. He would then go onstage and perform more or less extemporaneously. On one occasion, Lytton was so unsure of himself that he brought the text onstage with him, hoping to sneak a peak every now and then. "Well, Mr. Bundle?" he said to the other character onstage.

"Well," the other said in return.

"Well," stuttered Lytton.

"Well," replied Mr. Bundle.

A third "Well" from Lytton met with a third "Well" from Bundle.

The next "Well" came not from either of them but from the entire audience speaking as one person. "Well," the audience repeated impatiently, "say something."

Lytton, embarrassed, fled the stage and, in his agitation, left the text behind. When he ran back to retrieve it, he was met by an irritated shout of "Get off." He got off.

Fill in the missing words in these excerpts from well-known Gilbert and Sullivan songs:

A. From *H.M.S. Pinafore*

SIR JOSEPH PORTER:
When I was a lad I served a term
As office boy to an Attorney's firm.
I cleaned the windows and I swept the floor,
And I polished up the handle of the big front door.
I polished up that handle so carefulee

That _____ .

(nine words)

B. From *The Pirates of Penzance*

MAJOR-GENERAL STANLEY:
I am the very model of a modern Major-General,

I've _____ _____, _____, _____ _____,
I know the kings of England, and I quote the fights historical,
From Marathon to Waterloo, in order categorical;

(five words)

C. From *Iolanthe*

PRIVATE WILLIS:
I often thinks its comical—Fal, lal, la! Fal, lal, la!
Now Nature always does contrive—Fal, lal, la! la!
That every boy and every gal
That's born into the world alive

Is either a _____ _____

Or else a _____ _____!

(four words)

D. From *Patience*

BUNTHORNE:
If you're anxious for the shine in the high aesthetic line as a

_____,

You must get up all the germs of the transcendental terms, and
plant them everywhere.

(four words)

E. From *The Mikado*

NANKI-POO:
The flowers that bloom in the spring
 Tra la,
Breathe promise of merry sunshine—
As we merrily dance and we sing.
 Tra la,
We welcome the hope that they bring
 Tra la,

Of a _____

(five words)

Hawkeye Hijinks

A young trombone player with an excellent technique but very little background in orchestral performance was chosen by Arthur Nikisch to fill an opening in the Boston Symphony Orchestra. "Gentlemen," said Nikisch at the first rehearsal, "the opening work on the program is the Tchaikovsky Sixth. You all know it, so turn it over . . . " Before he could finish the thought, he remembered his new trombonist. "That is, I think you all know it. You," he said looking at the new player, "you know Tchaikovsky's Sixth Symphony, of course?"

The young man cleared his throat and declared forthrightly, "No, sir."

As the other players chuckled under their breath, Nikisch asked him whether he had at least heard it. Again the trombonist answered, "No, sir."

The conductor was so stunned that all he could manage to say was "I hope you enjoy it."

Meredith Willson, a flute player and future composer of *The Music Man*, claims that he, not the trombonist, was the subject of the above story. After graduating from high school in his native Mason City, Iowa, he came to New York City to continue his study of the flute under Georges Barrère, the distinguished first-chair player of the New York Symphony. Barrère used his influence to secure Willson a job with the New York Philharmonic. When the orchestra's first flutist fell ill, young Willson became the first-chair player for the next concert. The program included Beethoven's *Leonore* Overture No. 3. The conductor, Willem van Hoogstraaten, decided to forego rehearsing that piece because all of the musicians knew it so well. All, that is, except Willson, who knew almost nothing about serious music and whose only experience with ensemble playing had been as a member of John Philip Sousa's band. During the performance, the newcomer found himself unexpectedly playing a solo as all of Carnegie Hall watched and listened. When the piece ended, he sat back, and the audience applauded thunderously. Just as unexpectedly, the piccolo player next to him pushed him up and out of his chair to take a bow.

The next day, Willson told Barrère about the incident. Barrère was unable to contain his laughter. When he calmed down, he explained what had happened. Willson had winged it through one of the most famous solos in the entire orchestral repertoire.

Willson called his first book of reminiscences *And There I Stood with My Piccolo*. He borrowed his title from a story an old Moravian flute player had told him. Once upon a time there was a king, rich and powerful, who hired an entire orchestra to play for him because he felt lonesome. So delighted was he with the music that when the concert ended, he told the players that they could go into his countinghouse and fill their instruments full of gold. Pouch after pouch of yellow nuggets were squeezed into the bells of French horns and tubas and through the f-holes of violins and cellos. "And there," concluded the Moravian flutist, "I stood with my piccolo."

Hawkeye Hijinks
Iowa boy Willson makes good

116

Match the classically–trained composer on the left with the Broadway show on the right for which he knowingly or posthumously provided the score.

Leonard Bernstein – A   1 – *Anya*

Alexander Borodin – B   2 – *Apple Blossoms*

Edvard Grieg – C   3 – *Blossom Time*

Fritz Kreisler – D   4 – *Coco*

Jacques Offenbach – E   5 – *Helen Goes to Troy*

André Previn – F   6 – *Kismet*

Sergei Rachmaninoff – G   7 – *Magdalena*

Franz Schubert – H   8 – *On the Town*

Heitor Villa-Lobos – I   9 – *One Touch of Venus*

Kurt Weill – J   10 – *Song of Norway*

Foot-in-Mouth Disease

Another of the eminent conductors of the New York Philharmonic when Willson played there was the Dutchman Willem Mengelberg, famous for his lengthy rehearsal lectures. One day Willson was telling harpist Teddy Cella and a few other colleagues the story about the musician in the madhouse who had played under all of the great conductors in the world. In spite of being in the asylum, the musician was in complete command of his faculties except when the name of one particular maestro came up—Willem Mengelberg. Then, said Willson, "he became a slithering, slobbering, hollering hunk of lunacy."

To lend realism to his tale, Willson slid to the floor and began to scream hysterically. His audience seemed unimpressed. Willson's histrionics intensified. He writhed about and flapped his arms like some kind of demented bird-snake, and yet curiously, no one was laughing. As he got up and dusted himself off, he caught a glimpse of a familiar but distinctly unimpressed bystander. It was, of course, Mengelberg.

Eventually, Willson struck out on his own as a radio bandleader. In 1941 he stopped off in Detroit to guest-conduct a program called "The Ford Sunday Evening Hour." Met soprano Eleanor Steber and pop singer Lanny Ross were engaged as soloists. The event happened during a period in Willson's life when he was displaying an

More Hawkeye Hijinks
Willson lays an egg

unfortunate penchant for saying the wrong thing, which weighed heavily on his conscience. Happily, the broadcast went well, after which the participants withdrew to the home of Ford executive Cyril Bottom for cocktails and went from there to a country club for dinner. Willson, Steber, and several others arrived at the club lobby at about the same moment that Mr. and Mrs. Bottom showed up. "Aha! Mr. and Mrs. Bottom," exclaimed Willson, proud of remembering their names.

"Well!" Mr. Bottom cried. "How clever of you to remember our names! What is your secret?" asked a delighted Mrs. Bottom.

Willson answered, "It's very simple—I always connect a name with a face."

Frantically, Steber excused herself and joined another group. Willson joined the army.

An Electronic Grease Monkey

After the war, Willson found his talents as musician and personality much in demand in the electronic media. He was a regular on an early Mark Goodson and Bill Todman–produced TV game show called "The Name's the Same." He also led the band for a couple of radio programs, "The Big Show" and "Encore." In addition to Willson, the stars of "Encore" were the Met's Robert Merrill and Marguerite Piazza, each of whom was required to contribute five or six songs or arias per program. Everything was going smoothly with "Encore" until one day Merrill's out-of-town commitments made it impossible for the popular baritone to go on. Just when it looked as though they would have to do a show without him, someone got a bright idea. The show's engineers would record Merrill's voice unaccompanied and then play back the tape during the broadcast with Willson's band behind it.

And it was done. A recording studio was emptied except for Merrill and the band's pianist, who was seated in a remote corner playing just loud enough to keep the baritone on key, but not so loud as to be heard on the tape. No sooner had Merrill caught a plane for Sioux City than someone made a disturbing discovery: the music was recorded about a halftone flat. The piano had been tuned low to accomodate some monkeyshines on comedian Morey Amsterdam's show that morning. Merrill had expressed some misgivings about the pitch, but ultimately chalked up the apparent lowness of it to a head cold he had been battling. Now what to do? The first suggestion, to lower the accompaniments a semitone, had to be discarded when it was realized that the piano had been lowered not a full semitone but somewhat less. Eventually, the recording department came to the rescue again. An engineer got hold of the original tapes and arranged to speed them up by hand while the show was on the air, having only his ear, his nerve, and an incredibly steady hand to guide him. Not a single listener noticed anything unusual.

Because the procedure had to be kept secret, the heroic engineer could not come forward for commendation. The following week, however, a small sign Scotch-taped to the recording department door puzzled those at the station who weren't in on the secret: WE FIX FLATS.

119

A noticeable difference in casting between Broadway and European opera is that on Broadway, the leading man is usually a baritone instead of a tenor.
Match the baritone on the left with the Broadway show on the right that he starred in as a member of the original cast.

Alfred Drake – A   1 – *Do I Hear a Waltz?*

Sergio Franchi – B   2 – *Annie Get Your Gun*

Ray Middleton – C   3 – *Oklahoma!*

Ezio Pinza – D   4 – *The Unsinkable Molly Brown*

Harve Presnell – E   5 – *South Pacific*

Match the baritone on the left with the Hollywood version of a Broadway musical he starred in on the right.

Nelson Eddy – A   1 – *Carousel*

Howard Keel – B   2 – *Man of La Mancha*

Richard Kiley – C   3 – *Naughty Marietta*

Gordon Macrae – D   4 – *Show Boat* (1951 version)

Lawrence Tibbett – E   5 – *New Moon* (first version, 1930)

Ludwig the Louse

One of Oscar Levant's lifelong ambitions was to make Hollywood more appreciative of good music. Once a producer went with Oscar to an all-Beethoven concert because the man wanted to become known as a deep thinker. Despite these intentions, he was plainly relieved when the last piece on the program came along. The piece was Beethoven's Fifth Symphony, whose final movement is marked by a series of false endings. At the first one, the producer stood up to leave. When the orchestra kept going, he seated himself. At the second one, the same thing happened. After the third such incident, he turned to Oscar.

"The louse fooled me again," he whispered.

Oversell

When the Czech composer Ernst Krenek arrived in Hollywood, George Antheil and friend Ben Hecht decided that Sam Goldwyn ought to hire Krenek to score a film Sam was planning that was to have a Czech background. After a strategy session, the boys marched into Sam's office and told him the good news: the leading composer in the world had just arrived in town.

The producer requested his name.

"Krenek."

"Never heard of him," Sam said. He wanted to know what this musical marvel, this Klinick or whatever his name was, had written.

George cited *Jonny spielt auf*, an opera that enjoyed a brief but spectacular vogue in Weimar Germany.

Sam had never heard of this *Jonny spielt auf*. Still interested, he asked what else Klotnick had done.

The complete list of Krenek's well-known works now exhausted, George mentioned *The Threepenny Opera*. Yes, sir, Ernst Krenek had definitely composed the immortal *Threepenny Opera*. Ben seconded it, nodding confidently.

The Selling of Ernst Krenek
He wrote Faust, La traviata, Der Rosenkavalier, The Threepenny Opera—*practically everything anybody's ever heard of*

But Sam hadn't heard of *The Threepenny Opera* either.

Undiscouraged, one of the boys said something about *Der Rosenkavalier*. Ben told Sam that, yes, Krenek had written the stupendous *Rosenkavalier*, an opera that in Europe in the preceding year had brought in a fortune.

Sam took heart. He thought that on sunny days with the wind blowing from left to right he had heard of this whatchacall *Duh Rosencavalry*.

Faust. Seemingly from out of nowhere, *Faust* entered the conversation. Ernst Krenek had written *Faust*, too.

Now Sam was really impressed. *Faust* was a work he knew and loved. The Czech composer was beginning to look like a shoo-in for the job.

To apply the finishing touch, Ben threw in *La traviata*. Among Ernst Krenek's many timeless masterpieces were *Der Rosenkavalier*, *Faust*, and *La traviata*.

At the mention of Verdi's opera, Sam's mood suddenly darkened. His face, sunny a moment ago, turned positively cadaverous. The producer ordered George and Ben to bring Klinick or whatever his name was to his office so that he could have the pleasure of tearing him limb from limb. Krenek's—Verdi's—publisher, it seems, had socked Goldwyn with a near-fatal lawsuit because a film of his had quoted without permission a few measures from *La traviata*.

Backpedaling from Sam's ire, George and Ben made for the door, realizing that they had fallen into the trap of overselling their product.

QUESTION
52 **Name one famous musical work that can be heard in each of the following films.**

A _____ *Elvira Madigan*

B _____ *2001: A Space Odyssey*

C _____ *Ordinary People*

D _____ *Moonstruck*

E _____ *The Seven-Year Itch*

Fiddling and Diddling

Film composer Dimitri Tiomkin was always on the lookout for ways to curry favor with producers. An important filmmaker had a distant in-law who was a chronically unemployed violinist. Tiomkin knew what to do. He got the man a permanent position in the fiddle section of a Tiomkin-led studio orchestra. Mordecai Pinsky was his name. At the next recording session there was Pinsky. And there Pinsky remained for many years to come.

One day Tiomkin wanted to show one of the studio's executives how a certain tune went and decided to summon a violinist and pianist to play it. The violinist was Pinsky. When told what Tiomkin wanted, Pinsky became panic-stricken and began looking around the room for help. He raised his fiddle to his chin, but was unable to produce anything that sounded remotely like a correct note.

Through the years, the other violinists in the orchestra had covered for Pinsky, who only went through the motions, never touching the violin's bow to the strings.

A Revealing Climax

One of Tiomkin's best friends was the film director Frank Capra. During the Second World War Capra was in Hollywood, where he produced morale-boosting *Why We Fight* documentaries. Needing background music for his series, Capra hired Tiomkin to write and arrange it. Of all of *Why We Fight*'s emotionally charged installments, the Ukranian-born composer found the most moving to be the one depicting the battles for Russia. Capra and his staff collected reams of Soviet was footage illustrating the German invasion and the Russian resistance. For Tiomkin, the siege of Leningrad summoned so many memories of names and faces in happier times that he couldn't prevent himself from crying.

As a composer, he rose to the occasion. He whipped up a dramatic potpourri of themes from the Russian masters and scored it for an oversize orchestra and chorus. Neither the army's orchestra not its sound stage were large enough for it to be performed as written. The air force's orchestra also had to be put to work for the performance, which was given at the spacious Paramount studio.

Tiomkin was swept away by the occasion. He threw himself into the music, exuberantly but carefully bringing in instruments and chorus to sculpt thrilling climaxes. Suddenly, as he and the music swelled with fervor, he felt something snap. It was his belt. Amid the savageries of war before him, laughter exploded incongruously behind him. Ordinarily earnest and stolid officers were rolling in the aisles. Tiomkin's pants had fallen to his ankles and now he was standing in shirttails and underwear. A viola player removed his belt and handed it to him, after which Tiomkin turned around at the conductor's stand and in his broken English apologized: "Sorry for having unfortunate accident. Damn belt broke, which should not happen. Great embarrassment, but I'm laughing too."

QUESTION 53

Match each of the following film composers with the group of films for which he provided scores.

A. Elmer Bernstein

B. Bernard Herrmann

C. Maurice Jarré

D. Erich Wolfgang Korngold

E. Alfred Newman

F. Miklós Rósza

G. Max Steiner

H. Dimitri Tiomkin

I. Franz Waxman

J. John Williams

_____ 1 *King Kong, Gone with the Wind, Casablanca, Now Voyager, A Summer Place*

_____ 2 *Bride of Frankenstein, Rebecca, The Philadelphia Story, Sunset Boulevard, A Place in the Sun*

_____ 3 *Street Scene, The Hurricane, The Song of Bernadette, The Robe, Anastasia*

_____ 4 *Captain Blood, Anthony Adverse, The Adventures of Robin Hood, The Sea Hawk, King's Row*

_____ 5 *Jaws, Star Wars, Superman, Raiders of the Lost Ark, E.T.*

_____ 6 *The Man with the Golden Arm, The Sweet Smell of Success, The Magnificent Seven, To Kill a Mockingbird, The Grifters*

_____ 7 *Citizen Kane, The Ghost and Mrs. Muir, North by Northwest, Psycho, Taxi Driver*

_____ 8 *Double Indemnity, Spellbound, The Lost Weekend, The Killers, Ben-Hur*

_____ 9 *Lost Horizon, High Noon, The High and the Mighty, Friendly Persuasion, The Alamo*

_____ 10 *The Longest Day, Lawrence of Arabia, Dr. Zhivago, Is Paris Burning?, Ryan's Daughter*

6

Opera

Your Magic Sword—
Do Not Leave Home without It

What singer turned in the greatest performance of all time on the operatic stage? Relatively few permanent records survive, and so much is a matter of personal taste that even to consider the question is futile.

But curiously, one individual performance does stand out, not for its aesthetic aspects, but as an example of determination triumphing over adversity in the grand "the show must go on" tradition. The singer was Curt Taucher, a Wagnerian tenor who sang at the Metropolitan Opera in the twenties and early thirties.

It all began on a Saturday afternoon during a production of *Siegfried*, with Taucher singing alone on stage clad in the title character's brief and ragged costume. As he sang, a trapdoor opened and clouds of smoke billowed dramatically onto the stage. Taucher finished his solo triumphantly but took one step forward too many and —whoosh!—down he plunged through the trapdoor opening. Down, down thirty feet down the chute went the unfortunate tenor, accumulating as he fell all the dirt and grime that had collected during years of inattention.

Before you could say "Richard Wagner," Taucher hit the basement floor, scaring the hell out of the workers down there. Fearing he might have killed himself, they ran to his assistance and picked up something that looked like an oversize dust mop perched atop a couple of wobbly legs. But Taucher sprang to life, muscled his way past them, and sped to the elevator, shouting as he went, *"Mein Schwert! Wo ist mein Schwert?"* ("My sword! Where is my sword?") Perhaps he wished that the magical powers of Siegfried's sword, Nothung, would carry over into real life.

As the smoke continued billowing, all backstage was pandemonium. Calls went out for the workers to break Taucher's fall, for a physician, for the general manager, for the assistant general man-

An Unexpected Visit from Taucher the Tenor
The thrilling start of Siegfried's Slide Journey

ager, for everyone and everything that anybody could think of. Walter Jagemann of the Technical Department raced downstairs with a first-aid kit and a glass of smelling salts but, to his shock, ran into a frightful-looking Taucher coming out of the elevator. The singer, knowing no English, grabbed the ammonia thinking it water and, without even blinking, guzzled it down. Would he drop dead now? wondered Jagemann. No! the indomitable Taucher began trotting toward the stage with Jagemann jogging alongside, frantically beating the dust out of his costume. In the wings a stagehand gave him a sword. *"Mein Schwert!"* he shouted joyfully, as though everything were now back to normal.

And, sure enough, right on cue, as though he hadn't almost done himself in twice, Taucher returned to the stage to finish out the opera. The smokescreen had hidden his disappearance from an unsuspecting audience.

After the last curtain call, an amazed group including the general manager swarmed around the tenor backstage to tell him how wonderful was his performance. It was then that Taucher discovered that he had not escaped scot-free. As he shook hands he grimaced. He had broken his little finger.

The Meeting of the Twain

Diva Olive Fremstad, majestic and unpredictable, specialized in Wagnerian heroines at the Met a generation or so before the better-known era of Kirsten Flagstad and Helen Traubel. Her stage career ended in 1917 when the Met banned opera sung in German following America's declaration of war against the Kaiser. Fremstad's final days were spent at Little Walhalla, the bucolic retreat she built for herself in Bridgton, Maine, in the heart of that state's lake region. There her well-intentioned efforts at befriending the locals met with success, but not without a breaking-in period.

Madame Fremstad and her lady-in-waiting went out for food and ice one day to the farmhouse on the hill, where they discovered the ladies' sewing circle meeting in the front room. The hostess offered them handsome portions of cake and ice cream, which they glee-fully devoured while sunning themselves on the porch. The singer then walked inside to meet the women and sat down at the melo-deon, where in gratitude she sang "Comin' through the Rye," "Auld Lang Syne," and a favorite Scandinavian folk song.

The ladies were stunned. They applauded with the hesitant, des-ultory applause of those who have just been thunderstruck by the sound of an unexpectedly wonderful instrument. A voice like Ma-dame's had never been heard around those parts, to say nothing of inflections that endowed everyday sentiments with profound feel-ing and drama. Clearly they had to make some additional show of interest. Madame was in the kitchen when one of the ladies—appar-ently the "character" among them—stuck her head in the doorway and said, wagging a finger, "Before you go, mind you, we want some more of that singing!"

The ever-growing width of Madame's glowering eyes reflected indignation raging in her heart. She pulled herself up to her most intimidating height and responded haughtily, "Woman, have you any idea what you ask?"

Name the sopranos.

A. The post-Fremstad generation of Flagstad and Traubel pro-duced another remarkable Wagnerian soprano, one whose singing was matched by her courage and determination.

She was born in 1909 in Australia, studying there prior to moving to Paris to further her training. A successful début at the Met in 1935 was followed by a performance as Brünnhilde in

Madame Fremstad Issues a Refusal
Do not ask for seconds on divine favors

Götterdämmerung that netted her considerable publicity. For the Immolation Scene, she leapt onto a horse that charged into the funeral pyre, thereby becoming the first soprano since 1881 to follow Wagner's stage directions so faithfully. But during a rehearsal of *Die Walküre* in Mexico City in 1941, she found herself unable to get off a couch or even move her muscles. It was polio. An intense period of physical rehabilitation followed, culminating in her making a series of professional appearances in the concert hall and on the operatic stage from a sitting position. She sang Isolde at the Met on March 24, 1944, from a carefully camouflaged wheelchair. Her autobiography, *Interrupted Journey,* was filmed in 1955 with Eleanor Parker in the central role. She passed away in 1979. Who is she?

B. Eleanor Parker's singing in that picture was dubbed by a soprano famous for her versatility.

She was born in Connecticut in 1920. Her professional career began in 1941 when she dubbed in a few measures of "Home,

Sweet Home" for a documentary on NBC radio. This led to an engagement on a weekly radio program, the success of which earned her her own radio program. She made her television début on "The Milton Berle Show" in 1950.

The fifties saw her career as a classical musician in full swing as she made numerous appearances in the concert hall and on the operatic stage. Among her significant recordings was one in 1952 as one of the soloists in Toscanini's reading of Beethoven's Ninth Symphony. It was in 1960, the year she made her Met début in Gluck's *Alceste*, that the full range of her versatility became evident. She made a record that became a bestseller. It was not one of operatic arias or classical repertoire, but one of popular song standards. It was called *I've Got a Right to Sing the Blues*.

Still active in the nineties, she recently made a series of recordings for Reference Records with small combo showcasing standards by some of America's best-known songwriters. She is perhaps the most stylish pop chanteuse who was originally an operatic diva. Who is she?

An Unusual Compliment

The hefty contralto Ernestine Schumann-Heink did not know how to define fame except by citing specific examples. A person is famous, she said, when he or she has an experience such as the one that happened to her.

It occurred in 1927. She was staying in a ramshackle hotel in some one-horse town in the American West. A grizzly old tobacco-chewing cowpoke seated next to her in the lobby spotted and looked her over with a knowing eye.

"Say, ma'am," he said, spitting out some tobacco juice, "ain't you that big, fat, famous female singer whose face we're a-seein' all the time in the newspapers?"

"Well," Schumann-Heink replied, "I'm a big, fat female, I'm sorry to say, and I'm a singer, I'm sure of that—but about being famous way out *here*—"

"Oh, yes," the other interrupted, "yes, yer are! I know yer—know all about yer! You're the one we're always readin' about. Why, we git our papers out here 'most every week—and thar was a pictur in the last one looks jest like yer. Oh, you're the one I mean—and no mistake! You're her, all right!"

Madame considered that the greatest compliment that had ever been bestowed upon her. Even by a grand duke.

Schumann-Heink and Friend
"Ain't you that big, fat . . . singer?"

The above is reminiscent of something that happened around the turn of the century ot the concert pianist Ossip Gabrilowitsch. Gabrilowitsch sat down in the dining car of a train taking him from one engagement to another on a concert tour of the American West. A porter came to his table, filled his water glass, and said to him, smiling broadly, "Nice to see you, sir."

Gabrilowitsch, startled at first, was flattered by being recognized under those circumstances. He said to the man, "You know me, then?"

"Yes, sir," said the porter. "You're the gentleman that takes no ice with his water."

Trio-stan and Isolde

Winter can play havoc with the Met's personnel. Birgit Nilsson had just scored an enormous triumph as Isolde and was looking forward to another night's performance in that same role. But vocal problems were troubling her leading man, Ramon Vinay, who felt unable to sing the arduous role of Tristan with only four days' rest. "All right," thought Met manger Rudolf Bing, "if Vinay can't make it, why don't I try Karl Liebl?" He phoned Liebl; Liebl had a cold. Sir Rudolf looked at his watch. Four o'clock. Only one tenor remained whom he could ask to sing Tristan: young Albert Da Costa. He phoned Da Costa; he, too had a cold. What to do?

"If none feel up to singing the entire opera," wondered the resourceful manger, "maybe each could sing just one act."

Happily, the idea was agreeable to the four principals—Nilsson and the three tenors. The house lights went down and Bing stepped before the curtain, summoning a huge groan from the audience, who feared that he might be about to announce the cancellation of La Nilsson. The manager told them that La Nilsson was fine. A collective sigh of relief. The problem was with Tristan. A smaller groan. Sir Rudolf declared that the Met had three outstanding Tristans, all of whom were physically subpar. But against their physicians' advice, all three, to save the performance, had consented to sing one act each. Laughter rang out in the house. When Bing added that fortunately *Tristan* had only three acts, the laughter turned into a roar. But the day was saved.

All but one of the following are conspicuous and recurring motifs taken from famous operas. Four are from Wagner's *Ring*, but the fifth is found in a popular opera by another composer. Which is it?

QUESTION
55

A. Sword motif

B. Death motif

131

C. Reflection motif

D. Fate motif

E. Renunciation of love motif

A Bouncy Tosca

Puccini's *Tosca* ends when the title character leaps to her death over a prison wall, on the other side of which a mattress is always positioned to cushion the soprano's fall. Stella Roman was seized by fright before a performance and ordered two extra mattresses placed behind the parapet. La Roman jumped, only to have the mattresses boomerang her back onto the stage. Puccini had failed to write something to cover this emergency, leaving the singer no choice but to leap a second time.

Seeing Red

Tosca in Cleveland provided Beverly Sills with her most colorful impersonation. William Chapman as Scarpia, for the stabbing scene, carried a celluloid capsule to crush against his chest to suggest blood. When the big moment arrived, Chapman unfortunately pointed the capsule in the wrong direction and sprayed the fake blood all over Sills's face, teeth, and hair. The audience began to chuckle; so did Chapman. Sills had labored hard to heighten and provide the tension, and she wasn't about to allow it to dissolve in mirth. A well-placed kick at Chapman put a stop to his merriment and allowed the act to continue without incident. But a full thirty minutes were required to get the soprano scrubbed off for the third act.

Getting Even

Grace Moore sang *Tosca* in Corsica with a crafty old bass as her Scarpia. Everything went well during rehearsals. Scarpia would always place Moore solicitously on the divan for the rape scene to enable her to be in condition to sing "Vissi d'arte." But his conduct at the performance was an altogether different matter. He threw her to the floor so hard that breathlessness made it impossible for her even to whisper, let alone sing. The temperamental soprano was now in a mood for revenge. She recognized her opportunity at the end of the second act, the scene in which Tosca slays Scarpia and places a crucifix on his chest.

Before the next performance, Moore shopped around and managed to find a crucifix that weighed almost thirty pounds. Near the end of the act she dropped it not onto Scarpia's chest but directly onto his groin. The singer shouted curses and then lay so immobile that Moore thought she had actually murdered him. But the bass remembered who he was—an opera star. He responded to the curtain call, taking deep bows. Although the audience was calling for Tosca, Moore refused to take her bows until she had first made sure that she had her manager on one side of her and her chauffeur on the other.

Which one of the following contains a statement about Puccini that is *false*?

QUESTION
56

A. All but one of Puccini's twelve operas have been mounted by the Met, giving him the highest percentage of production there of any composer who wrote primarily for the stage.

B. Puccini became interested in making an opera out of the play *Madame Butterfly* after attending a production in London of which he, a non-English speaker, couldn't understand a word.

C. Puccini and his publisher, Ricordi, successfully sued Al Jolson for infringement of copyright, claiming that Jolson's song "Avalon" stole from one of the composer's best-known arias.

Grace Moore's Revenge
Proven effective for evil spirits, vampires, and uppity basses

D. Puccini's opera *Suor Angelica* is unusual with respect to casting; its cast is composed entirely of men.

E. Puccini's *Girl of the Golden West* bears little resemblance to the Jeanette MacDonald–Nelson Eddy musical film of the same name, which discarded Puccini's music in favor of an original score by Sigmund Romberg.

Misfires

One of opera's most frequently botched scenes occurs in the first act of Verdi's *La forza del destino*. In the story, Leonora is discovered by her father alone with her secret lover, Don Alvaro. To signal his peaceful intentions, Alvaro throws his pistol to the ground only to have it discharge accidentally, killing his sweetheart's father. At a performance in Havana in 1920, the stagehands failed to produce the necessary gunshot sound at the appropriate moment, forcing Enrico Caruso, in the role of Don Alvaro, to shout *"Buuum!!!"* Caruso started laughing, whereupon the audience laughed too, thereby relaxing everyone and assuring the success of the performance.

Beniamino Gigli, Caruso's successor at the Met, firmly refused to sing *La forza*, believing that it had been hexed by someone possessing the evil eye. But he finally broke down and attempted the part in 1939 in Buenos Aires. Everything went off without a hitch until the pistol-throwing scene. In this production, the gunshot was to have been produced onstage by a prop-hidden stagehand firing an airgun. As Alvaro, Gigli threw down the gun, but no shot was heard. The father fell to the floor anyway. Someone backstage—not the stagehand with the airgun—realizing that something had been left out, decided to lend plausibility to the proceedings. So about thirty seconds after it should have happened, a shot rang out. Gigli's fears were realized.

In *Un ballo in maschera*, Renato is supposed to kill Riccardo with a pistol. But for reasons that can easily be imagined, a dagger is often substituted for the gun. Despite the possible difficulties, Met director Herbert Graf decided to revive the pistol for the new production of the opera. Everything went off satisfactorily at the final rehearsal, but afterward, as apprehensions grew, Graf decided to play it safe and go back to using a knife. When Robert Merrill as Renato stabbed Jussi Bjoerling as Riccardo, a technician unaware of the final arrangements produced the unmistakable sound of a gunshot. Gun or knife, it made no difference to Bjoerling. The only decent thing for a man in his position to do was to fall down and die.

Identify the operas of which the following are summaries of the plot or basic situation:

A. _____

This must have been a favorite of Gilbert or Sullivan or both, inasmuch as it involves baby swapping, a favorite device of theirs. It includes a gypsy hag named Azucena, her "son" Manrico, a minstrel knight who is actually the kidnapped child of the elder Count di Luna, and the beautiful Duchess Leonora, who is loved by Manrico and the younger Count di Luna, his natural brother.

B. _____

The Czech national opera, this concerns the lovers Mařenka and Jenik, a poor youth, and their attempts to remain a couple despite her parents' determination to find a wealthy match for her through the medium of the local matchmaker, Kečal.

C. _____

Belmonte is in search of his beloved Constanze, who has been kidnapped by pirates acting on behalf of Pasha Selim, in whose household she now resides. When an elaborate escape plan goes awry, Belmonte is recognized as the son of his worst enemy by Pashe Selim, who frees Belmonte and Constanze when he decides he will no longer return evil for evil.

D. _____

Nadir and Zurga are fishermen and friends in love with Leila, a virgin priestess who is now not to be approached or seen by human eyes. When Nadir is caught having a clandestine romance with her, he is condemned to the stake by the high priest but subsequently freed by the fisher king Zurga, who realizes that in an earlier adventure Leila had protected him from his mortal enemies at the risk of her own life.

E. _____

Max, a proud forester, must win a shooting contest tomorrow in order to gain the hand of Cuno's daughter, the fair Agathe. He falls in with a black arts dabbling forester of sinister aspect named Caspar, who invites Max to join him at midnight in the Wolf's Glen, where they will forge several bullets to use in the contest.

Taken to School

Robert Merrill, though he does not believe in false modesty, finds the exciting life he has led almost incredible. How difficult it is for him to realize that the fat, stammering lad of a few years ago has become a great opera star.

The public's admiration for him and his work never ceases to amaze him. He received a phone call after a radio interview from a fan who said that she had all of his records and deeply appreciated his singing. She apologized if she had disturbed him, but just *had* to let Merrill know what a great admirer she was of his. The caller was the legendary Geraldine Farrar. Merrill was astounded.

When Merrill and his wife went to see Paul Muni perform, Merrill sent a note backstage asking the great actor to allow them to pay their respects. Muni's reply was quick and eager. It happened that he, too, was an admirer of Merrill's.

Naturally, an artist of international eminence such as he is besieged on all sides by autograph hounds. Merrill was once taken unawares by a little girl in a classroom converted into a dressing room.

"All right, young lady," he said impatiently in a why-fight-it tone. "What do you want my autograph on?"

"Nothing," she answered. "I came in here to feed my snake."

A Cheeky Musetta

In a performance of *La Bohème*, Robert Merrill as Marcello once hugged Ljuba Welitsch as Musetta and, as directed, in a moment of playfulness tossed her into the air. The dynamic Welitsch's skirt flew up around her head, revealing everything but a pair of panties. The prompter gulped. A livid manager, Sir Rudolf Bing, sped backstage and told her never, never to do that again. Ljuba the redheaded bombshell did not believe in wearing underwear onstage or, it was whispered, off.

Welitsch Baring Up under Stress
For husbands who sleep at the opera, food for thought

As a longtime headliner at the Met, Merrill was a frequent performer on its Saturday afternoon radio broadcasts. Answer the following questions about this long-running program.

A. _____ Who is its sponsor?

B. _____ Who is its current announcer, or who was its announcer from December 25, 1931, until December 30, 1974?

C. _____ What activity is featured during an intermission on every broadcast?

D. _____ Who is the host of this segment?

E. _____ What pianist and opera producer for years had a near-weekly intermission segment devoted to opera commentary and analysis?

Vintage Bruno

Some artists devote so much time to their work that they arrive at stardom without being able to cope with the simplest demands of everyday life. Such was the case with Bruno Landi, a tenor who sang for many years at the Met and Covent Garden. So problem prone and insecure was Landi that he always wore a tag beneath his shirt indicating his name, address, and phone number. Even crossing the street was too terrifying for him. He would stand on the corner and wait for someone to help him across.

He and Robert Merrill signed for a performance of *The Barber of Seville* in Mexico City, an engagement that brought out what might be described as Vintage Bruno.

The fun started on the flight down. The tenor sat directly in front of Merrill. Landi produced a couple of rosaries and began praying as the plane taxied for takeoff. Several times he turned around, his face awash with perspiration, to make sure that Merrill was still behind him. Merrill could get out of his seat whenever necessary only by pulling back on the one in front—Landi's. "Help! The plane is crashing!" Landi would scream.

The tenor managed to calm down a little, but told Merrill that for the landing he needed a couple of air sickness bags. They went unused. Merrill led Landi by the hand at the terminal to the customs station, where the baritone presented his passport. Landi's was missing. It was not on his person. It was not in his luggage. He began crying uncontrollably, hysterically, begging the arriving security police between sobs not to clap him in prison, where he would surely die.

Merrill hightailed it back to the plane, where he found the passport on the floor in front of Landi's seat. The two left the airport and without incident checked into their hotel. They faced the issue of dinner now and the threat of Montezuma's revenge, which plainly troubled Landi. What could he safely eat? Merrill found the shiniest, most salubrious-looking restaurant in town, only to have Landi tell him he couldn't eat a thing. Chicken had small bones in it that would surely asphyxiate him. Pork would give him trichinosis, liver heartburn. Salad would result in the worst gas attack since the Battle of Verdun. Landi ordered beef broth.

Merrill managed to lead his charge by the nose through the next two days, finding a barber to shave him, a hotel valet to dress him, and so on. Before the nine o'clock performance, the two had dinner at four, during which Landi, eating his chicken broth, began choking. The tenor told Merrill that in the morning he had had a frog in his throat, and that now he absolutely had to find a voice teacher to get his voice back into shape before the curtain tonight. Otherwise, no performance. A voice teacher who spoke English, a language Landi somewhat understood, was eventually found—on the other side of town, of course. Merrill and Landi took a cab to the studio. There the baritone excused himself, but not before arranging to have Landi take a taxi back to the hotel after the lesson. As luck would have it, Landi and his cab driver became hopelessly lost. Merrill eventually managed to steer them to their destination thirty minutes before the opening by having a Mexican phone operator talk to the Mexican cabby.

The curtain went up at 10:30, an hour and a half late. Landi was largely responsible. Merrill was putting the finishing touches to his makeup when he heard the tenor in the next room screaming. In this he was not alone. The theater manager and his assistants had him surrounded and were yelling threats in Spanish back at him. There was one fear that Bruno Landi, despite all his insecurities, had overcome—that of asking for his fee. He was asking for it now and absolutely refused to set foot on the stage until he got it. And he wanted no more back talk, because in the present uproar he was losing his voice.

The warring parties removed Landi's fee from the theater's cash box, and Merrill sewed it into his costume. The performance went passably well until the scene in which the Count (Landi) serenades

139

Rosina to the accompaniment of Figaro's (Merrill's) guitar. As Merrill, in keeping with custom, faked the introduction on the guitar, Landi strode over to him, turned his back to the audience, and stuck out his tongue. He told his Figaro that he was sick. His tongue was all red and he couldn't possibly sing.

Merrill took a few deep breaths as an involuntary reaction of disbelief. He whispered to Landi that Bruno, you absolutely *have* to sing.

Impossible, physically impossible, Landi droned in reply.

Merrill began strolling around onstage to the music of the guitar as Landi followed him, insisting that he was ill. Tears began rolling down his face. The audience noticed some of this and thought that it was all a part of the opera. The able, confident Figaro was showing the reticent Count how to be bold.

All at once, Merrill felt overwhelmed. All of the frustrations and inconveniences of the past two days hit him in the head like a ton of bricks. *Two* tons. He had gotten Landi this far and wasn't going to allow him to ruin the opera after everything. Merrill told him that

Robert Merrill Curing Bruno Landi's Vocal Problems
Physical therapy did the trick

140

he was going to sing or, goddammit, he was going to break this frigging guitar over his frigging head.

Merrill lifted the instrument quickly with his left hand and with his right spun the tenor around. The first note of the accompaniment was played offstage as the guitar began its downward descent. Bruno burst into the sweetest serenade this side of heaven.

QUESTION

59

Rossini's *Barber of Seville* (1816) replaced the once popular 1782 treatment by Giovanni Paisiello in public estimation in the same way that Verdi's *Otello* made people forget a successful earlier version.

Name a composer who also wrote an opera based on the subject treated in any one of the following.

A. _____ Massenet's *Manon*

B. _____ Puccini's *La Bohème*

C. _____ Puccini's *Turandot*

D. _____ Gounod's *Faust* (as *Mefistofele*)

E. _____ Gounod's *Faust* (as *Doktor Faust*)

F. _____ Mozart's *Don Giovanni* (as *The Stone Guest*)

G. _____ Wagner's *Die Meistersinger* (as *Hans Sachs*)

It Still Beats Cursing the Darkness

A new Met production of *The Barber of Seville* added some stage business for a lamplighter. The lamplighter's reponsibility was to ignite two street lights at opposite ends of the stage by touching them with a long pole. The touching of a light was to signal to an electrician backstage.

The lamplighter on opening night reached up for the lamp on the left, but the electrician for some reason lit up the one on the right. When the right one was touched, on went the left. The lamplighter, to overtake the electrician, began frantically racing back and forth. Amid rising laughter, Robert Merrill entered to discharge Figaro's famous "Largo al factotum." The audience sympathized with the victimized performer, and Merrill met with a tumultuous ovation.

Rossini's *Barber* is, of course, based on the celebrated play by Beaumarchais.

All of the following serious operas are based on prestigious literary works as well. Which one was *not* composed by Rossini?

A. *Don Carlo*

B. *La donna del lago*

C. *Mosè in Egitto*

D. *Otello*

E. *Tancredi*

Down But Not Out

The chubby mezzo-soprano Minnie Hauk had a problem maintaining her balance during a performance of Bizet's *Carmen*. In the first act, with her hands tied behind her back, Carmen attempts to arouse Don José by swaying seductively back and forth while seated on a three-legged stool. Hauk swayed too much forth and not enough back, and fell ignominiously off the stool. The plump singer then faced the most difficult part of her performance: getting up from the stage with her hands tied behind her. Somehow she managed to get up, right the stool with one leg, and sit down again, but not before sputtering an English word ending in *-ing* followed by a noun.

When portraying Escamillo in performances of *Carmen* at the Met, the young Robert Merrill used to steal a page from Douglas Fairbanks's book: he would always precede the swaggering "Toreador Song" with a majestic leap onto the table at Pastia's. On tour one night, the stagehands forgot to jam a wedge against the table's wheels. Merrill rocketed into the wings in superb voice and then calmly walked back, completing the song without missing a beat.

Carmen may be the most popular opera in the world at the moment. Answer the following questions about this Bizet perennial:

A. _____ What Spanish city provides the location for the first act?

Robert Merrill as Escamillo
Giving new meaning to 'on wings of song'

B. _____ What is Carmen's profession?

C. _____ Ethnically, what is Carmen?

D. _____ To what animal does Carmen compare love in the first line of her Habañera?

E. _____ From whom does Micaëla in Act I, Scene 2, bring a message for Don José?

F. _____ Carmen tells Don José that she will do two things when she goes to the tavern of her friend Lillas Pastia. Name one.

G. _____ When Carmen in Act II, Scene 3, sings and dances for Don José, her voice is accompanied by two musical instruments, one of which she plays herself. Name them.

H. _____ To what part of the country do Carmen and Don José run away?

I. _____ With what kind of outlaw band do they consort?

J. _____ What popular event happens on the day that Don José kills Carmen?

143

Relieving the Tension

Enrico Caruso was a jolly soul who couldn't resist the opportunity for a good practical joke. Sometimes he would stand backstage during the overture and wiggle his ears in time to the music. He and baritone Giuseppe de Luca once were fined for squirting water pistols from the wings at soprano Frances Alda as she bent over to pick up something during a performance of *Otello*. On another occasion, Nellie Melba, imperious queen of opera, extended her hand to him while he sang "Che gelida manina" ("What a cold hand"). Caruso stuffed it with a warmed-up sausage roll that, when she recoiled, bounced erratically across the stage.

But even Caruso was subject to stage fright. The future playwright Laurence Stallings, who played a Nubian slave in *Aida*, wrote a detailed report about Caruso's movements before a particular performance at curtain time. He observed that as Caruso chain-smoked, a fireman would trot after him picking up the butts that he discarded. His big aria, "Celeste Aïda," was coming up soon, and the tenor was nervous. For situations like this he kept in his brass belt a vial of mouthwash. Caruso approached Aïda's throne, next to which Stallings was standing, and made a gesture as if to say "Lord, what heavenly beauty!" with clasped hands holding the vial. Then he turned his back to the public, took a big swig of the mouthwash, spat it all over Stallings, turned around, and began "Celeste Aïda."

QUESTION
62

Which *one* of the following statements about Enrico Caruso is false?

A. Caruso excelled in the French repertoire as well as the Italian, but sang very little German opera.

B. Caruso was an extraordinarily successful recording artist; his rendition of "Vesti la giubba" in 1902 became the first record to sell more than a million copies.

C. Caruso was the successful defendant in what was called "the monkey house case," in which improper behavior toward a woman was alleged while looking at the animals in Central Park Zoo.

D. Caruso spent nearly the last twenty years of his life in the United States, where he married an American heiress.

E. Caruso played himself in the film biography of his life.

An Unexpected Singing Coach

After making his radio début, Metropolitan Opera tenor Beniamino Gigli was uneasy. He felt that, psychologically and technically, he was not suited to that particular medium but, to abide by his contract with NBC, he kept at it. After another radio performance, Gigli was engaged in conversation by a young elevator operator. The boy asked the tenor if he were the guy who had just sung on the radio. Gigli's secretary translated for the singer what the lad had just said, including the word "guy." Then the youngster asked Gigli if he would mind getting a little advice. Gigli said no, he did not mind. The boy told him that his voice was coming over too loudly because he was standing too close to the mike. Gigli smiled appreciatively and thanked him for the pointer. The boy told him not to mention it. He was used to straightening out "amateurs."

Are you a "G" whiz? You will have the correct answer when you say "Gigli" if you are ever asked to name Enrico Caruso's successor at the Met. But can you fill in these blanks?

QUESTION

63

A. G_____ Famous Vivaldi choral work, or Meathead's spouse.

B. G_____ Scottish conductor Alexander, or what you get when you garnish gin and dry vermouth with pearl onions.

C. G_____ The third movement of Prokofiev's *Classical Symphony*, or *My Fair Lady*'s "Ascot ————."

D. G_____ Ravel's piano suite consisting of "Ondine," "Le gebet," and "Scarbo" (four words).

E. G_____ *Appalachian Spring* choreographer, or forties sportscaster McNamee.

F. G_____ Fux counterpoint treatise, or the first movement of Debussy's *Children's Corner* (three words).

G. G_____ Opera by Ponchielli, or Huxley smile.

H. G_____ *On the Mall* composer, or famous disillusioned American anarchist.

I. G_____ Founder of Russian musical nationalism whose name sounds like wrong note played on a piano.

J. G_____ *Exodus* composer, or the kind of record every recording artist wants.

K. G_____ Humperdinck heroine, or 1962 Australian America's Cup challenger.

L. G_____ Johann Strauss baron, or Styne-Sondheim Merman Broadway vehicle, or destructive moth.

M. G_____ Famous Bach keyboard variations, or Gertrude Berg role, or *Ghost* star.

N. G_____ Verdi heroine, or 1946 Hayworth film vehicle, or gal who wished she could shimmy like her sister Kate.

O. G_____ Beethoven's Piano Trio No. 4, or George or Marian Kirby.

P. G_____ Mezzo Simionato, or love interest in Act III of *Tales of Hoffmann*.

Q. G_____ Terra firma, or cheap beef, or a pattern of notes repeated over and over again in a musical composition.

R. G_____ Fiordiligi's *Cosi* boyfriend, or radio inventor Marconi.

S. G_____ Scottish soprano (1877–1937) friend of Debussy, or where the Celts play.

T. G_____ Eighteenth-century operatic innovator, or soprano Alma, wife of Zimbalist.

U. G_____ Composer Schuller, or Hagen's half brother in *Götterdämmerung*.

V. G_____ *Latin American Symphonette* composer, or Streisand ex.

W. G_____ Harmonica Mozart wrote for, or minimalist composer Philip.

X. G_____ Adam ballet, or fifties "Your Hit Parade" chanteuse MacKenzie.

Y. G_____ Beaux Arts Trio cellist Bernard, or supposed 'global warming' effect.

Z. G_____ Pitcher Lefty, or a small orchard of fruit-bearing trees, or the Beethoven and Schubert expert who founded an authoritative encyclopedia of music.

An Evenhanded Resolution

Donizetti's *Maria Stuarda* was announced for La Scala in 1835 with Anna del Serre and Giuseppina Ronzi–deBegnis, two singers who hated each other, scheduled to play Elizabeth and Mary. The confrontation scene, rehearsed with the composer in attendance, lived up to its name in more ways than one. Ronzi, in the role of Mary, approached del Serre in the role of Elizabeth and called her a vile bastard and an obscene, worthless whore. Del Serre was sensitive on these subjects and felt Ronzi's aspersions were cast much too vehemently to be mere acting. Enraged, she grabbed Ronzi by the hair and, according to one account, slapped her around, bit her, and kicked her to the point of nearly breaking her own foot. Ronzi, stunned at first, rallied so effectively that she knocked del Serre to the floor, senseless.

Ronzi, thinking Donizetti out of earshot, cried out that the composer was protecting del Serre. But Donizetti kept his cool and reminded his singers who they were portraying. "*They* were both whores," said he, not caring how much he distorted history, "and *you* are both whores." Admonished, they stopped squabbling and returned to their roles.

The post–Second World War revival of interest in bel canto singing exemplified by the works of Donizetti, Bellini, and Rossini resulted in the return of several operas based on historical sources.

QUESTION

64

All but one of the following historical operas were composed by Donizetti. Which one?

A. *Anna Bolena*

B. *Nabucco*

C. *Dom Sébastien*

D. *Lucretia Borgia*

E. *Roberto Devereux*

One Mustn't O.D.

Jan Peerce's roots were in popular music. As a young man, he entertained vacationers in the Catskills with a dance band in which he played the violin and sang under the name of Pinky Pearl. Steady work singing in theaters led to a regular spot on the airwaves on "The Radio City Music Hall of the Air." That, in turn, led to his becoming a regular fixture as well in that theater's stage show.

Peerce's mother, a somewhat straitlaced lady, visited her son only three times at Radio City. Several years had elapsed after the second call when, unexpectedly, she showed up backstage. Peerce had turned down a wedding invitation from a cousin of his, and she had come to ask him to reconsider.

"Is that what you came all the way here for?" Peerce asked, astonished. He explained that he hardly knew his cousin and promised to send him a nice present.

But his mother was a believer in family and wouldn't let the matter rest. So forcefully did she insist on his attending the wedding that he realized that any further resistance on his part would have been useless.

"All right. I'll go to the wedding if it'll make you happy," he sighed. "Now do you want to stay and see the show?"

"No," she said. "I saw it a couple of years ago." And she went home.

Quid Pro Quo

Mario Lanza's popularity was soaring in the late forties after the release of his first starring motion picture, *The Toast of New Orleans*. The tenor was now booked by an Asian impresario for a Hawaiian tour, on which he was expected to enchant audiences with his usual mix of opera and light classics. One thing remained to be done before leaving for the tour. As an expression of gratitude, Lanza and his wife, Betty, entertained the impresario and his American spouse in the Lanza home in the presence of Sam Weiler, his manager, who was putting the finishing touches on the itinerary. Food and drink were abundant. The impresario's wife asked for a look at the upstairs. Lanza agreed to show it to her. He gave a confidant who was present the signal he always gave whenever he wanted to prevent people from walking in on him in an intimate position.

The upstairs tour finished, Weiler informed Lanza that the impresario had cheated him on commissions and that nothing could be done about it.

"Forget it, Sam," said Lanza wearing a big smile. "Don't worry. He screwed me, I screwed his wife."

Match each of the following tenor arias with the opera and the situation in which it occurs.

A. "La donna è mobile"

B. "Nessun dorma"

C. "Vesti la giubba"

D. "Questa o quella"

E. "Recondita armonia"

F. "E lucevan le stelle"

G. "Ecco ridente in cielo"

H. "Il mio tesoro"

___ 1 In Verdi's *Rigoletto*, the Duke's first-act song, in which he says that to him all women are delightful and that to remain faithful to one of them will never be his intention

___ 2 In the same opera, the Duke's song in the last act, in which he declares that all women are hopelessly fickle

___ 3 In Mozart's *Don Giovanni*, Don Ottavio's florid second-act aria, in which he says that he is about to avenge Donna Anna's wrongs by slaying the murderer of her father

___ 4 In Leoncavallo's *I pagliacci*, the clown Canio's aria in which he comments on the irony of his situation: he must laugh and make his audiences roar with mirth even though his wife recently ran away with another man

___ 5 Count Almaviva's first-act serenade in Rossini's *Barber of Seville*, in which he beckons his darling Rosina to arise now that dawn is breaking and come to the window

___ 6 In Puccini's *Tosca*, the artist Cavaradossi's first-act aria, in which he says that the painting of Mary Magdalen on which he is at work was inspired by his ardor for Tosca

___ 7 In the same opera, the now-imprisoned Cavaradossi's third-act aria, in which he recalls his former bliss with Tosca

___ 8 In Puccini's *Turandot*, Calaf's third-act aria, in which he says that not only will none of the princess's subjects sleep tonight, as she commanded, but she won't either as long as she continues to ponder the profound mystery of his identity

Don't Call It Stingy, Call It Economical

The high C's of Francesco Tamagno, Verdi's first Otello, were said to have been so powerful as to make Covent Garden's chandeliers shake. Tamagno commanded fabulous fees, but was subject to incongruous gestures of economy. He and Nellie Melba were both guests of honor at a dinner given by the Millionaires' Club of New York. The soprano had heard tales of the tenor's resourcefulness and didn't have long to wait to witness examples at first hand.

Melba kept quiet, keeping an occasional eye on Tamagno. Then it happened. The tenor, seated next to the Italian ambassador's wife, spread out a napkin on his lap and began looking about himself with the eyes of a glutton. Calmly, as though it happened every day, he began dropping glazed fruits, salted almonds, and chocolates onto the napkin.

The time came for the women to leave the table. Tamagno arose too. He reached for an orchid bouquet that the women had been given and said with a bow that he would like to give it to his ailing daughter back at the hotel.

Only women having hearts of leather could refuse a request like that. He was allowed to take the bouquet.

Melba dined with Tamagno again at a luncheon given by the conductor Luigi Mancinelli at a New York Italian restaurant. The

Tamagno and Melba
Not even the stare of a prima donna assoluta *could keep him in line*

bill of fare included veal cutlets milanese, of which a few were left over. Tamagno, seeing that no one else wanted them, heaved a huge sigh of relief. He summoned a waiter and asked for a newspaper. The tenor told Melba, Mancinelli, and the others as he wrapped the meat that he had a little dog at home whose favorite repast was just these very cutlets.

Mancinelli called on Tamagno at his hotel the following day. The tenor and his daughter were sitting down to eat. Between them was Tamagno's makeshift doggie bag.

Sing a Song of Crisco

Turn-of-the-century tenor Leo Slezak was in Houston for a production that gave him the chance to play his most celebrated role, Otello. It had a most unusual playbill, one that included a plot summary that began as follows:

"OTHELLO"
Opera in Four Acts
by
Giuseppe Verdi
Act I

The people of Cypria are on their knees praying for the safe passage of their beloved Otello, whose ship is caught in a tempest. The weather clears. Otello disembarks and greets his people by saying:

USE CRISCO, THE BEST SHORTENING

"Rejoice! The Turks are defeated and drowned in the sea." The people salute Otello.

CRISCO IS UNSURPASSED

Iago, jealous of Otello, tries to make him drink. A drinking song

CRISCO HAS NO RIVAL

follows during which the intoxicated Cassio attacks Montano. Otello intervenes and cries out:

CRISCO IS ECONOMICAL

etc.

Identify the following operas by Giuseppe Verdi:

A. _____ Which Verdi opera was commissioned by the Khedive of Egypt?

B. _____ Which opera of his about a hedonistic duke is based on a play by Victor Hugo entitled *Le roi s'amuse*?

C. _____ Which Verdi opera has a much-praised libretto written by a fellow composer? (choice of two)

D. _____ Which opera of his exists in two versions, which have altogether different settings, one of which is Boston?

E. _____ Which Verdi opera includes a gypsy named Preziosilla who sings a rousing refrain in praise of war?

Evidence of the Law of Gravity

Francis Alda was very particular about her appearance. A performance of *La Bohème* with Caruso had her outfitted with pantaloons beneath a long skirt. When she bent down to fetch something, her garters popped, and down to her ankles went her undies. Alda, looking like a duck, waddled behind a couch and stepped out of them. Caruso, always on the lookout for a laugh and singing in full voice, picked them up, bowed to the lady, and spread them out for the learned inspection of the public.

Alda with her pantaloons wasn't as lucky as her contemporary Blanche Marchesi, who, singing Santuzza in *Cavalleria rusticana* at Covent Garden, felt something coming undone during the church scene with Turiddu. In the story, Turiddu has to enter the church from which Santuzza is banned as a sinful excommunicant. In order to conceal what was happening to her apparel, the desperate Marchesi violated the intention of the librettist by jumping into the church. She threw the troublesome garment to an astonished stage manager, jumped back out, and fell weeping on the steps of the church.

Also reminiscent of Alda's pantaloons is the experience of a famous English soprano during a production of *Cavalleria rusticana*. As she lofted her high A flat during the passionate duet with Alfio, her upper row of teeth fell out. The baritone, whose motives were less benign than Caruso's, picked up the teeth and put them on the table in full view of the audience.

Cavalleria Rusticana in England
A lovely performance all gummed up

Pietro Mascagni is remembered outside of his native Italy for only one opera, *Cavalleria rusticana*. Match the opera composer with the one and only work for which he is widely known.

Albert Lortzing – A   1 – *The Beggar's Opera*

Otto Nicolai – B   2 – *Czar und Zimmermann*

John Christopher Pepusch – C   3 – *La gioconda*

Amilcare Ponchielli – D   4 – *The Merry Wives of Windsor*

Ermanno Wolf-Ferrari – E   5 – *The Secret of Suzanne*

In *The Secret of Suzanne*, listed above, what is the secret that makes Suzanne's husband suspect that she is having an extramarital affair?

Why Ruby Keeler in *Forty-Second Street* Is Looking Better Every Day

Erich Leinsdorf was a young maestro with the San Francisco Opera when its general manager was Gaetano Merola. Leinsdorf came upon Merola in the chorus room one afternoon listening to Canio's familiar melodies in *Pagliacci* being sung by a short, chubby man whom he did not recognize. Merola waved Leinsdorf to sit and listen as he continued to coach the hopeful singer to give more of this and less of that. The general manager dismissed the man ten arduous minutes later with the vehement command to study, study, study *hard*.

The aspiring singer was a motorcycle cop named George Stinson. Stinson had sung a few Irish ballads about a year earlier at a stag gathering at the Bohemian Grove, an exclusive club frequented by Merola and his friends. So impressed were they with the Irish tenor that they believed they had discovered a Hibernian Caruso. Spontaneously they had collected enough money to stake Stinson to a six-month period of study in Milan. There, they hoped, he would acquire the skill and polish necessary to net him offers from La Scala, the Met, and the world's other prestigious opera houses.

But in Milan, Stinson had found it difficult to keep his mind on voice training. It ran, as the minds of red-blooded young men often will, to spaghetti, spumante, and skirts. Now here he was, at the San Francisco Opera six months later, his début in *Pagliacci* only three weeks off.

The dress rehearsal found Stinson so unprepared that Merola had to schedule an unprecedented second full dress rehearsal for the following evening. Then the début! Every company member not performing that night made sure he or she had a box seat to watch the local motorcycle cop stride across the stage singing and acting and beating Canio's big drum.

Was it nerves? Or simply a case of a young man being ignorant of his strength? When Stinson-Canio reached the center stage, he struck the drum so forceful a blow that his drumstick, fist, and forearm plunged through one drumhead, shattered the other, and emerged on the other side. Try as he would, the unfortunate man could not extricate himself from the drum. What happened next we do not know. Leinsdorf, our source for this event, headed for the nearest bar. It took him months to get up the courage to ask about Stinson. He was told when he did that the young cop was back on his motorcycle.

George Stinson as Canio
After this, chasing killers was child's play

Leoncavallo was inspired to write *I pagliacci* by the success of Mascagni's *Cavalleria rusticana*. The two are often spoken of in the same breath, paired on the same bill, and recorded together. They are perhaps even more closely linked in the public mind than the three operas of Puccini's *Triptych* (*Il trittico*), which are not performed and recorded together nearly as frequently as the operas commonly known as "Cav" and "Pag."

Which of the following threesomes compose Puccini's *Triptych*?

QUESTION

68

A. *La Bohème, Madame Butterfly,* and *Tosca*

B. *Le villi, Edgar,* and *La rondine*

C. *Il tabarro, Suor Angelica,* and *Gianni Schicchi*

D. *Il tabarro, Tosca,* and *Turandot*

E. *La rondine, La Bohème,* and *Le villi*

155

Snuffed Out

Violinist Thomas Ryan was playing in the pit in Glasgow in a long-forgotten opera whose characters included a robber. A reward was offered for the robber's head, and he was duly captured and decapitated. The next act opened with the severed head sitting on a table covered by a floor-length valence. Through a hole in the table protruded the actual head of an actor seated on the stage, the same actor who had earlier played the robber. His services were required to lend the scene an illusion of reality. The gallery gods now were tired of the whole opera and figured out a way to express themselves. They secured some very old, strong Scotch snuff and, through a blowpipe, wafted it downward toward the stage. The head sneezed and sneezed and sneezed, banging its chin on the table with each downstroke. With that, the opera closed.

Snuffing Out a Long Run
Quit while you're ahead

Off the Beaten Path

Gustav Mahler was once a young conductor of opera in the German town of Laibach (now Ljubliana in Yugoslavia). The soprano for a production of *Martha* failed to show up for the rendering of "The Last Rose of Summer." Mahler filled in for her. He turned around from the podium and, in his customarily precise, melodious tones, whistled the song.

The same theater lacked the personnel necessary for the Soldier's Chorus in *Faust*. A lone singer subbed for a platoon of uniformed men by parading around the stage warbling the Lutheran hymn "A Mighty Fortress."

The above led us to reflect that an essential ingredient in a successful production is a sympathetic audience. The late nineteenth-century diva Emma Albani relates an incident at secondhand that put its audience in a decidedly less than sympathetic mood.

Don Giovanni was about to be staged, for which, of course, a man on horseback and a property horse were required for the statue scene. Nothing could be found to serve as the horse except a small one made of wood and canvas about the size of a donkey. The man mounted the horse and was told to remain perfectly still except for the moment when he had to bow his head. He was long-legged, and his feet rested on the floor when he was astride the horse. The absudity of the spectacle was enough to undermine the composure of the audience. But things got worse. Midway through the scene in which the man was to remain motionless, he let out with a lusty sneeze, destroying the scene and sending the audience into hysterics.

Name the operatic sources of the following:

A. _____ The Dance of the Seven Veils

B. _____ The Hymn to the Evening Star

C. _____ The Ride of the Valkyries

D. _____ The Prize Song

E. _____ The Anvil Chorus

F. _____ The Polevtsian Dances

G. _____ The Hallucination Scene

H. _____ The Bell Song

Don Giovanni in the Provinces
A not-so-commendable Commendatore

Dublin Trouble

The Dublin premiere of *Faust* in 1863 was a grand occasion. Advance reports from London about opera and cast had raised expectation to a fever pitch. But the momentousness of the event did not prevent the gallery gods from entertaining each other between acts with a little lyricism of their own. One was a determined chap who regaled his fellows with an air that drew so much attention as to hold up the third-act curtain. The audience downstairs began to get restless, as did the manager, James Mapleson. Mapleson ordered the curtain rung up, whereupon a storm of protest erupted in the gallery, forcing it to be lowered again. The song concluded, a voice from the gallery calmly informed everyone down below that that section was now ready for Act III. Up went the curtain. After a series of signals from the stage Mephistopheles was supposed to emerge through a trapdoor. The first yank on a bellpull indicated "make ready," the second "send him up," and the third "lower him down." Mapleson, upset to the point of distraction by the intermission's celestial antics, gave the first pull and left. The stage manager appeared a second later and gave what he thought was the sign to make ready, only to have Mephistopheles pop up prematurely. The next pull was given and down went the unhappy singer just as he was about to start singing. His efforts at getting himself raised up came to naught. Marguerite throughout the rest of the scene had to fend for herself.

QUESTION 70

Many operatic numbers are commonly referred to by a title, such as Leporello's "Madamina! Il catalogo e questo," which is known as the Catalogue Aria. Few if any repertory operas contain as many vocal numbers that are known by a title as does *Faust*.

Name two vocal numbers in *Faust* that are commonly referred to by title.

_____

_____

A Stylish Pantomime

Musicians sometimes forget the most essential aspect of performing—showing up. Playing des Grieux in a production of *Manon* in Amsterdam, baritone Jess Walters tried to get his son to leave the seminary and rejoin secular life. When the scene was set to begin, the son for some reason never appeared. Walters, keeping his cool, sang to an empty chair as though his son were actually there, even persuading the invisible offspring to sign an important document. Audience and management were so delighted with the baritone's skill and sangfroid that he was signed for a long season.

QUESTION 71

Who Am I?

I am the Italian-born founder of the French national opera. As the son of one milliner and the grandson of another on my mother's side, my origins were humble, a fact I considered an unwanted encumbrance when I began to penetrate the highest royal circles. As a child in my native Florence, I learned the elements of music—from a Franciscan monk, some said—as well as skill on the guitar and, above all, on the violin. But it was my charming singing voice that secured my entrée into a better

Jess Walters's Stylish Pantomime
Tenors—who needs 'em?

world. In 1646 the Chevalier de Guise heard me and, when I was thirteen, brought me to France at the request of his niece, the Mademoiselle de Montpensier, in whose household I remained in various capacities until I was twenty. My talents as a dancer and mime tickled the fancy of no less a personage than the young Louis XIV himself, which prompted me to ask for my release from my lady's service. I got it. It was December 1652 and I was now living in Paris.

Two months later, His Highness and I danced together in the same ballet for the first, but by no means the last, time. (Around the powerful, I knew how to be complimentary, submissive, witty, or charming as the situation required.) How great was my fortune a short time later when the court composer for instrumental music passed away and a search began for someone to replace him. I was that someone. In 1661 and 1662 more important appointments followed. In July of the latter year, I was named music master to the royal family. Among those who a few days later signed my contract of marriage—to the daughter of a well-connected musician, incidently—were Louis XIV and Queen Anne themselves. Yes, the stumpy, guitar-picking milliner's kid with the funny accent had definitely arrived.

160

Now I began to seek out the most famous playwrights in France to collaborate with me on modest stage works. In 1669 a poet named Perrin was awarded a twelve-year royal monopoly to set up opera houses anywhere in France. I denounced him and them and asserted that my adopted language was unsuitable for lengthy stage works. But I sang a different tune three years later when Perrin went broke and I purchased the monopoly from him. Now no stage work that was sung throughout could be performed anywhere in the realm without my written permission.

I was in control and I wanted everyone to know it. I even decided at one point that marionette shows couldn't be given with music. The poor dears.

No longer did I go in search of France's most eminent play-wrights—Corneille, Moliere, et al. Now they came in search of me. Even the fabulist La Fontaine came to me, libretto in hand. When I refused him, he turned around and attacked me in an infamous diatribe entitled *The Florentine*, calling me, among

Who Am I?
"Around the powerful, I knew how to be complimentary, submissive, witty, or charming as the situation required"

other things, lewd. (Yes, my tastes often ran to members of my own sex, but is that *lewd*?) Anyway, it didn't matter. It took him a while, but he apologized.

Another, Guichard by name, came to me with a text and an offer of ten thousand livres. When I told him that his offer wasn't good enough, he tried to arrange for my premature demise by having a confederate garnish my snuff with arsenic.

From 1673 to 1686, to keep everyone happy—everyone that had to be, that is—I was good for one opera, or *tragédie lyrique*, a year. I carefully composed the choruses and the important ensembles and left busywork such as filling in the inner voices to my understudies Collasse and Lallouette. When it got back to me that the latter was bragging that not I but he wrote the best airs in my delightful *Isis*, I calmly told him in my Florentine accent so many used to laugh at that his services were no longer required.

At length, my works came under attack from the clergy and the Sorbonne. They were espousing immortality, they said. Even my old friend, His Majesty, was beginning to have his doubts. Fine, I said. From now on, I will write church music. Who would have thought that such a lofty resolve would lead to my undoing? One day, during a performance of my *Te Deum*, which I wrote to celebrate His Majesty's recovery from an operation, I accidently stabbed my toe with the tip of the walking stick I used to beat time. An abcess developed and then, when I refused the sawbones permission to amputate, gangrene. I put my wordly affairs in order and made my peace with the church before departing this world on March 22, 1687, leaving five houses, 800,000 livres, a flock of offspring, and a grieving widow who somehow arranged for the construction of a stately mausoleum in my honor.

Now, I ask you, how can a man who is housed forever in that kind of building, and who can command that degree of loyalty from that kind of woman, have been *lewd*?

Who am I?

Why Czarist Russia Fell

Gregor Piatigorsky tells about touring Czarist Russia with the Bolshoi Opera Orchestra. Breathless advertisements spoke of a huge precision orchestra numbering in the hundreds; in fact the ensemble numbered only seventeen, which called for some unusual doubling when the company performed Tchaikovsky's *Eugene*

Onegin in Samara. Mr. Jubansky, conductor, for example, was also the orchestra's French horn section. He cut an unusual figure by standing absolutely motionless on the podium with his horn held to his mouth. Piatigorsky had in front of him not one but four stands, his own cello part plus parts for clarinet, oboe, and trumpet, which he was also supposed to play.

Meanwhile, the lead tenor, Mr. Susow, as manager of the company, was concerned that the lady who was to sing the role of Tatiana, a virginal country girl, showed up in an advanced state of pregnancy. Another problem was a vodka bottle sticking out of the pocket of the double bass player, who stood near Piatigorsky.

Mr. Jubansky mounted the podium with his French horn and began. The overture went satisfactorily, but not so the opera. As incident piled on incident, the audience became increasingly restive. Matters came to a head when suddenly Susow, in the middle of his aria, inexplicably stopped. The conductor, desperate for a substitute, pointed to the double bass player with the vodka bottle and shouted, "Sing!" The bass player dutifully began, but got only as far as "Olga, goodbye forever!" when he pitched forward in a drunken stupor and with his double bass crashed into the surrounding instruments. At this point, the audience stampeded the box office like a horde of angry cossacks and shouted, "We want our money back!"

The Bolshoi's *Eugene Onegin*
The pregnant virgin was the least of their problems

The Public Speaks

The atmosphere surrounding operatic performance in some locations in the last century was a bit like that at a baseball game.

Operas in Barcelona were performed whole unless cuts were formally announced beforehand. A bass named Colonnese was singing Macbeth in Verdi's opera despite having a voice that was too high for the part. He made it through the entire work except for the Romance in the next-to-last scene, which he attempted to skip. The audience noticed this and whispered among themselves until at last some disappointed "gallery god" cried out for the Romance. Other voices joined in, and soon a regular chant was in progress. The call boy came out after the curtain rang down to explain that Señor Colonnese never sang the Romance, did not know it, and could not comply with the request. But the audience remained adamant. It continued clamoring for the Romance and would not go home until it had heard it. Out again came the call boy. Señor Colonnese would be willing to accede the audience's request if he could bring the music with him. Why sure, everybody yelled. With the music or without it made no difference to them. The curtain rose and out came a rather contrite-looking Colonnese, score in hand, to plow through the piece. He was rewarded with a tumultuous round of applause. The opera reached its finale without further incident.

QUESTION

72 | Name the opera (answer *two* correctly).

A. _____ Baritone Leonard Warren dropped dead on the stage of the Metropolitan Opera on March 4, 1960, while singing in a production of what opera?

B. _____ What was the first opera to be performed at the Met?

C. _____ Part of what opera is performed in the Lon Chaney silent classic *The Phantom of the Opera*?

D. _____ During a production of what opera do the Marx brothers run amok in *A Night at the Opera*?

E. _____ When the diva fell ill at Paris's Opéra-Comique on April 10, 1900, voice student and future star Mary Garden was plucked from the audience to replace her and complete a performance of what opera?

Mademoiselle di Murska and Friends

The late nineteenth-century diva Ilma di Murska went to extraordinary lengths to avoid the city of Cologne because, she said, a German officer had once addressed her there before being formally introduced. This concern for formality even extended to her relationships with her pets. She traveled with a veritable menagerie. Her most expensive friends probably were a pair of parrots to whom she gave the freedom of her hotel room. When one of them passed away, the diva paid a handsome sum to find out whether it had been the victim of foul play. (It had not.) Mademoiselle also kept a monkey, an Angora cat, and a dog. This last was a huge Newfoundland that traveled in his mistress's coach after somehow stuffing

Mademoiselle di Murska Putting On the Dog
She told the press they were "just good friends"

himself beneath her seat. Pluto, as he was called, was a good-natured creature who dined daily with Mademoiselle. A place would be set for Pluto, and he would dine without allowing meat or bones to fall on either the floor or the tablecloth.

Call it Plutonic Love.

QUESTION
73

Match the soprano aria with the opera and situation from which it comes.

A. "Casta Diva"

B. "Caro nome"

C. "Ah, chi mi dice mai"

D. "Komm, Hoffnung"

E. "Mein Herr Marquis"

F. "O mio babbino caro"

G. "O patria mia"

H. "Sempre libera"

I. "Un bel di"

J. "Una voce poco fa"

K. "Voi che sapete"

_____ 1 In the second act of Johann Strauss's *Die Fledermaus*, a lively party is in progress at the villa of Prince Orlovsky. Among those present are Gabriel von Eisenstein and his chambermaid, in disguise and now calling herself Olga. When Eisenstein tells "Olga," with whom he has been flirting, that she looks just like a chambermaid he knows, she feigns indignation and asks how a lowly chambermaid could possibly have physical endowments like hers. She expresses this in an aria that is also known as "The Laughing Song."

_____ 2 Rosina's aria from the first act of Rossini's *Barber of Seville*, in which she discusses a secret voice, that of one Lindoro with whom she has become infatuated.

_____ 3 The aria that Cherubino the page sings in the second act of Mozart's *Marriage of Figaro*, in which he describes how he is tormented by pangs of young love.

_____ 4 Donna Elvira's entrance aria in the first act of Mozart's *Don Giovanni*, in which she wonders where the heartless reprobate is who wronged her so cruelly, adding that she would gladly forgive him should he change his mind and decide that he wanted her and her alone after all.

_____ 5 Norma's aria in Bellini's opera of the same name in which she prays to the chaste goddess of the moon to purge her fellow Druids of warlike emotions.

_____ 6 The aria in the second act of Verdi's *Rigoletto* in which Gilda, the title character's daughter, expresses her newly awakened feelings for a mysterious gentleman posing as one Gaultier Maldé.

_____ 7 In the first act of Verdi's *La Traviata*, Violetta meets Alfredo at a party at her home, finds herself falling for him, and toys with the idea of entering into a serious love affair. But, remembering what she is, a courtesan, she defiantly throws back her head and bursts into this aria, saying that she must remain unattached in order to flit from pleasure to pleasure.

_____ 8 In Verdi's *Aida*, the title character, held in captivity in Egypt, sings this early in the third act to express her homesickness for her native Ethiopia.

_____ 9 Cio-cio-san's aria in the second act of Puccini's *Madama Butterfly*, in which she expresses her faith that on one joyous day a ship bearing Lt. Pinkerton of the U.S. Navy, who married and abandoned her, will sail into Nagasaki harbor so that he can remain with her forever.

_____ 10 Lauretta's aria in Puccini's *Gianni Schicchi*, in which she pleads with her father, the title character, to allow her to marry the handsome Rinuccio.

_____ 11 Leonora's aria in the first act of Beethoven's *Fidelio*, in which she says that her eternal love for her imprisoned husband Florestan will ultimately give her the strength to rescue him from Pizarro's homicidal intentions.

Sobered by Experience

Some musicians have a very limited knowledge of music history. In the early years of this century, Leo Slezak was singing with a colleague named Baldwin whose knowledge was even more limited than most. Slezak couldn't resist playing a joke on him. During rehearsals of Gluck's *Armida*, Slezak brought out an elderly chap with flowing white beard, whom he introduced to the vulnerable Baldwin.

"Herr Baldwin," said Slezak, "I would like you to meet the composer of this marvelous music, Christoph Willibald von Gluck. Herr Gluck, Herr Baldwin."

Gluck, in reverent language, proceeded to thank the singer effusively for his superlative interpretation of his music. Baldwin was overjoyed with this praise from so eminent a musician and the next

Herr Baldwin Meeting Christoph Willibald von Gluck
He never knew when Mozart or Wagner would be out front

day couldn't wait to tell his colleagues about it. Loud was their laughter as they told him that Gluck had died well over a century ago.

Some time later, the same Baldwin was singing Canio in the company's production of *I pagliacci*. Into the director's box one evening came the opera's composer, Ruggero Leoncavallo, who happened to be passing through town. The production was a thrilling one. Leoncavallo went backstage at the conclusion and, in highly emotional language, expressed his deep appreciation to Baldwin. The singer asked the composer who he was. Leoncavallo, astonished at the question, told him that he was the composer of the opera just performed.

Baldwin, plainly annoyed, told him not to try *that* game on him. Lord knows how many centuries ago Leoncavallo had died!

With that, Baldwin stormed out of the room, leaving the composer standing by himself, open-mouthed.

Each of the following hypothetical operatic casts contains an error in either the year or in the choice of a singer to portray a particular role. Find the mistake in each.

A. _____ A performance of *Carmen* at the Met in 1992 starring Marilyn Horne in the title role, Samuel Ramey as Don José, Ileana Cotrubas as Micaela, and Sherrill Milnes as Escamillo

B. _____ A performance of *Rigoletto* at the Met in 1919 with Enrico Caruso in the title role, Frances Alda as Gilda, Louise Homer as Maddalena, and Giuseppe de Luca as Sparafucile

C. _____ A performance of *Faust* at Covent Garden in 1897 with Jenny Lind as Marguerite, Jean de Reszke in the title role, Ernestine Schumann-Heink as Martha, and Pol Plançon as Mephistopheles

D. _____ A performance of *Lohengrin* at the Met in 1946 with Lauritz Melchior in the title role, Birgit Nilsson as Elsa, Margaret Harshaw as Ortrud, and Desző Ernster as Telramund

E. _____ A performance of *La Bohème* at the Met in 1972 starring Mirella Freni as Mimi, Jussi Bjoerling as Rodolfo, Judith Blegen as Musetta, and Robert Merrill as Marcello

Back from the Dead

The 1919–20 season at the Met witnessed the production of a bid for The Great American Opera, Henry Hadley's *Cleopatra's Night*. One of the scenes called for Jean Gordon, as a slave girl, to stab herself and fall dead at the feet of Frances Alda, who sang Cleopatra. The stabbing at the dress rehearsal came off as planned, but instead of falling in place, Gordon at the premiere lost her balance and rolled down a row of stairs toward the proscenium. Her billowy chiffon dress was now mostly over her head, baring her legs and a sizeable portion of her torso. She calmly sat up, composed herself, and folded down her skirt. Only when she had assured herself that she was the picture of a model corpse did she lie back down and close her eyes again.

<table>
<tr><td>QUESTION
75</td><td>**Name the composers of the following American operas:**</td></tr>
</table>

A. _____ *Amahl and the Night Visitors*

B. _____ *The Ballad of Baby Doe*

C. _____ *Four Saints in Three Acts*

D. _____ *The Ghosts of Versailles*

E. _____ *The King's Henchman*

F. _____ *Nixon in China*

G. _____ *Porgy and Bess*

H. _____ *Vanessa*

Sheriff Bob

Soprano Lina Cavalieri was considered the most beautiful woman in the world. A regal, hourglass figure, combined with deep brown eyes surrounded by exquisitely classical facial features, made her every man's obsession. The humble flower girl turned Folies-Bergère singer toured Russia in 1900, where Prince Bariatinsky, son-in-law of Czar Alexander II, fell giddily in love with her and soon proposed. For her début in Saint Petersburg, the smitten prince arranged for her carriage to ride on a red carpet several blocks long that extended from her hotel to the theater. She loved mingling with Russian aristocracy, but left Bariatinsky after a short time when she decided to pursue opera worldwide. Her profession brought her to New York City, where she met and married her second husband, the fabulously wealthy socialite Winthrop (Bob) Chandler.

Chandler, for his part, had everything that practically every woman wanted. Tall, handsome, fun-loving, rich, and socially prominent, he was even artistically inclined as an accomplished screen painter. Folks called him Sheriff Bob. Chandler had a house on Long Island's Nassau County at a time when voters expected men from his social class to run for public office. Dutifully he ran for sheriff and won.

Sheriff Bob's wedding present to La Cavalieri was his mansion in Paris. Within a week of the wedding, she locked him out. Her taste for Russian aristocracy resurfaced, and now she invited Prince Dolgorouki, whose family history was as impressive as Bariatinsky's, to replace Sheriff Bob.

This nuptial disaster made headlines all over the world and produced a catch phrase that was repeated everywhere. Some time before, the Chandler family had been divided by a property dispute, which had been resolved by declaring one of Bob's cousins insane and packing him off to an asylum. Sheriff Bob had had a hand in it.

But the cousin hadn't stayed put. He had escaped and fled to Florida, where he picked up a newspaper one morning and read about the swift end of Bob's marriage. He sent Chandler a telegram of but three words. It read:

WHO'S LOONY NOW?

ANSWERS

1. (d).

2. (b): The baton was introduced in Germany in the last years of the eighteenth century. Neither it nor anything else could have been introduced by Mendelssohn in 1849. He had passed away two years earlier.

3. (c): The idea originated with Henry Hadley, composer and associate conductor of the New York Philharmonic. Hadley brought his idea to Miss Gertrude Robinson Smith, a wealthy Berkshire resident who, acting upon the proposal, organized the Berkshire Symphonic Festival and hired Hadley and the New York Philharmonic to give the festival's first concert, which it did on August 25, 1934. The original site was not Tanglewood but a horse ring on a farm in Interlaken, Massachusetts. Dissatisfaction with Hadley's programming prompted the festival's management to turn to Koussevitzky and the Boston Symphony, which gave its first festival concert on August 13, 1936, under an enormous tent at a second site, the Holmwood estate of Mrs. Margaret Emerson in Stockbridge. Delighted with Koussevitzky, the festival's organizers realized that a third site would have to be found when the conductor insisted that concerts for the following season be given in a permanent structure. Koussevitzky and Miss Robinson Smith chose the Tanglewood estate of Mrs. Gorham Brooks and Mrs. Mary Aspinwall Tappan when it was offered to him for his use in the fall of 1936. The Tanglewood shed opened in 1938.

4. (e): The Boston Symphony Orchestra did not join the American Federation of Musicians until December 1942, one of the last major American orchestras to do so. The AFM had barred the orchestra from the radio and the recording studio and had refused to allow union soloists and conductors to perform with it. So dismayed was Koussevitzky with the orchestra's nonunion status that he had secretly undertaken negotiations with the New York Philharmonic to become its music director beginning with the 1943–44 season.

5. (a) 3; (b) 1; (c) 4; (d) 5; (e) 2; (f) 6; (g) 7.

6. (b): The Boston Pops was founded in 1885 by Henry Higginson, who four years earlier had founded the Boston Symphony Orchestra. The Pops's first conductor was Adolf Neuendorff. Fiedler's innovation was

the free summertime concerts on the Charles River Esplanade, which he initiated as the conductor of the Boston Sinfonietta in 1929, one year before his appointment as the Pops's music director.

7. (d) and (e): Toscanini was associate conductor (along with Willem Mengelberg) of the New York Philharmonic for the 1928-29 season and was then its sole head conductor from 1929 to 1936. The conductor recently named to head the Berlin Philharmonic was not Klaus Tennstedt but Claudio Abbado.

8. (e): Bernstein played a considerable amount of modern music during his tenure as music director of the New York Philharmonic, albeit of a less futuristic variety than that programmed by Boulez.

9. (a): Stokowski programmed a considerable amount of modern music and conducted the premieres of many twentieth-century works. His motives with respect to these premieres were called into question when the number of his second performances was compared with the number of premieres. With respect to (e), Stokowski's three wives were the pianist Olga Samaroff (née Lucie Hickenlooper), Evangeline Johnson, and Gloria Vanderbilt, all of whom came from wealthy families. Evangeline Johnson was a Johnson & Johnson pharmaceuticals heiress.

10. (a) Chicago; (b) Cleveland; (c) Pittsburgh; (d) San Francisco; (e) Buffalo Philharmonic.

11. (a) Ax; (b) accents; (c) angel; (d) Angelina; (e) Anton; (f) Adele (two *l*'s for Ms. Davis); (g) Addison; (h) Auer; (i) Anderson; (j) Alexander; (k) Adelaide; (l) arabesque; (m) allegro; (n) André; (o) *Air Power*; (p) Ashkenazy; (q) Adam; (r) Adler; (s) Arthur; (t) *Alpine*; (u) Alfred; (v) Arias; (w) Aurora; (x) Antarctica; (y) Anthony; (z) Arnold.

12. (a) 2; (b) 3; (c) 5; (d) 4; (e) 7; (f) 6; (g) 8; (h) 1.

13. (b), (e), (c), (a), (d): The three violin concerti (b) were composed in the second half of 1775 by the nineteen-year-old Mozart. *The Abduction from the Seraglio* (e) received its triumphant premiere on July 16, 1782, the year after the composer settled in Vienna, where he spent his final decade. *The Marriage of Figaro* (c) débuted in the middle of that decade, on May 1, 1786. Mozart was suffering from his final illness and had little more than two months to live when *The Magic Flute* (a) was first performed on September 30, 1791. The Requiem (d), on which Mozart was working at the time of his death, was completed by his student Franz Süssmayer and was first heard in 1793.

14. (a) 6; (b) 4; (c) 8; (d) 2; (e) 7; (f) 3; (g) 1; (h) 5.

15a. (b): Boccherini's perennially popular Minuet is the third movement of a String Quintet in E composed in 1771 and published in 1775. Percell's "Trumpet Voluntary" (a) was written by Jeremiah Clarke. The authorship of Haydn's Serenade (c), as it is sometimes called, possibly music's most famous string quartet movement, is still in doubt. Few believe it to have been written by Haydn. Haydn scholars Alan Tyson and H. C. Robbins Landon make a case for the composer Romanus Hofstetter. The three movements of Haydn's *Toy* Symphony (d) were taken from a longer cassation (a kind of serenade) by Leopold Mozart, the father of Wolfgang Amadeus Mozart. The toy instruments were added to the scoring by Michael Haydn, the brother of Franz Joseph Haydn.

174

15b. (c).

16. (c): Schubert's Symphony No. 8 in B Minor, the "Unfinished" Symphony, was composed in October 1822, six years before the composer's death, and then set aside. By no means is it the only fragment among Schubert's output.

17a. *Das Rheingold, Die Walküre, Siegfried,* and *Die Götterdämmerung.*

17b. (a) *Siegfried;* (b) *Das Rheingold;* (c) *Die Götterdämmerung;* (d) *Die Walküre.*

18. (a) 5; (b) 4; (c) 6; (d) 3; (e) 1; (f) 2.

19. (a) 5; (b) 3; (c) 1; (d) 4; (e) 6; (f) 2.

20. (a) 6; (b) 8; (c) 3; (d) 2; (e) 5; (f) 1; (g) 4; (h) 7.

21. (a) Smetana: String Quartet in E Minor; *My Country (Má vlast),* a series of six tone poems of which *The Moldau* is the most famous. (b) Weber: *Invitation to the Dance; Jubel* Overture; Concertone in E Flat for Piano and Orchestra, Op. 26; two clarinet concertos; Grand Duo Concertante for Clarinet and Piano, Op. 48; Konzertstück in F Minor for piano and orchestra, Op. 79; Quintet in B Flat for Clarinet and Strings, Op. 34; and Variations on a Theme from *Silvana* for Clarinet and Piano, Op. 33. (c) Wagner: *Siegfried Idyll; A Faust Overture.* (d) Bizet: Symphony in C; *Patrie* Overture; *Jeux d'Enfants.* (e) Gounod: "Funeral March of a Marionette," which Alfred Hitchcock chose as the theme music for his television series, "Alfred Hitchcock Presents."

22. Vladimir Dukelsky, better known as Vernon Duke.

23. (a) Mahler; (b) Gounod; (c) Mussorgsky; (d) Stravinsky; (e) Gounod.

24. (a): Debussy's work is based on a poem by the nineteenth-century French Symbolist Stéphane Mallarmé. The others were inspired by examples of visual art.

25. (e): The composers mentioned in the clue are, in order, Milhaud, Auric, Poulenc, Honegger, Tailleferre, and Durey.

26. (a) 6; (b) 5; (c) 2; (d) 7; (e) 1; (f) 3; (g) 4.

27. (a) 3; (b) 2; (c) 7; (d) 4; (e) 5; (f) 8; (g) 1; (h) 6.

28. (a) Copland; (b) Balfe; (c) Ives; (d) J. S. Bach; (e) Saint-Saëns; (f) Grofé; (g) Liszt; (h) Mendelssohn; (i) Johann Strauss, Jr.; (j) Enesco; (k) Mendelssohn; (l) Mozart.

29. (a) *Pathétique;* (b) "Moonlight"; (c) *Appassionata;* (d) "Funeral March"; (e) "Clair de Lune."

30. (a) 5; (b) 1; (c) 3; (d) 2; (e) 4.

31. (d).

32. (a): The Melody in F and the *Ocean* Symphony were written by the nineteenth-century Russian composer Anton Rubinstein.

33. (e): Joan Morris, who performs with her husband, William Bolcom, is a singer.

34. (a) 3; (b) 1; (c) 2; (d) 4; (e) 5.

35. (c): Mussorgsky's *Night on Bald Mountain* is an original orchestral work.

36a. Adagio, Andante, Moderato, Allegro, Vivace, Presto, Prestissimo.

36b. *pp, p, mp, mf, f, ff.*

37. (a) Cage; (b) Campion; (c) Carlos; (d) Carpenter; (e) critic; (f) Chadwick; (g) Charpentier; (h) Chavez; (i) Ciccolini; (j) Clemens; (k) Chopin; (l) Cassidy; (m) Conried; (n) Crumb; (o) cadence; (p) Corregidor; (q) Camille; (r) can-can; (s) canon; (t) caprice; (u) cabal; (v) Crooks; (w) coffee; (x) Campanella; (y) carnival; (z) chord.

38. (b).

39. (a) Isaac Stern; (b) Jascha Heifetz; (c) Fritz Kreisler; (d) Sir Yehudi Menuhin; (e) Eugene Fodor.

40. (d): *Liebestraum* was written by Liszt.

41. (a) clarinet; (b) piano; (c) cello; (d) flute; (e) violin; (f) oboe; (g) harp.

42. (a) piano; (b) violin; (c) cello; (d) trumpet; (e) guitar.

43. (a): the solo instruments are violin and viola.

44. (a). The solo instrument in (b) is the French horn; in (c), it's the celesta; in (d), the flute; and in (e) the soprano voice.

45. (d).

46. (a) 3; (b) 4; (c) 7; (d) 1; (e) 8; (f) 6; (g) 2; (h) 5.

47. (a) 5; (b) 4; (c) 1; (d) 2; (e) 3.

48. (a) 2; (b) 10; (c) 1; (d) 7; (e) 4; (f) 9; (g) 3; (h) 6; (i) 5; (j) 8.

49. (a) now I am the ruler of the Queen's Navee;
(b) information vegetable, animal, and mineral;
(c) little liberal little conservative;
(d) man of culture rare;
(e) summer of roses and wine.

50. (a) 8; (b) 6; (c) 10; (d) 2; (e) 5; (f) 4; (g) 1; (h) 3; (i) 7; (j) 9.

51a. (a) 3; (b) 1; (c) 2; (d) 5; (e) 4.

51b. (a) 3; (b) 4; (c) 2; (d) 1; (e) 5.

52. (a) Mozart's Piano Concerto No. 21 in C; (b) Richard Strauss's *Also Sprach Zarathustra*, Johann Strauss's *Blue Danube Waltz*, the Adagio from Khachaturian's ballet *Gayane*, and Ligeti's *Atmospheres* and Requiem; (c) Pachebel's Canon; (d) Puccini's *La Bohème*; (e) Rachmaninoff's Second Piano Concerto.

53. (a) 6; (b) 7; (c) 10; (d) 4; (e) 3; (f) 8; (g) 1; (h) 9; (i) 2; (j) 5.

54. (a) Marjorie Lawrence; (b) Eileen Farrell.

55. Motif (d) is from Bizet's *Carmen*.

56. (d): *Suor Angelica* is cast entirely for women.

57. (a) Verdi's *Il trovatore*; (b) Smetana's *The Bartered Bride*; (c) Mozart's *The Abduction from the Seraglio*; (d) Bizet's *The Pearl Fishers*; (e) Weber's *Der Freischuetz*.

58. (a) Texaco; (b) Peter Allen, Milton Cross; (c) an opera quiz; (d) Edward Downes; (e) Boris Goldovsky.

59. (a) Puccini and Auber each wrote a version; both were called *Manon Lescaut*; (b) Leoncavallo; (c) Busoni; (d) Boito; (e) Busoni; (f) Dargomyzhsky; (g) Lortzing.

60. (a) *Don Carlo* was written by Verdi.

61. (a) Seville; (b) a factory hand in a cigarette plant; (c) a gypsy; (d) a bird;

(e) his mother; (f) dance the seguidilla and drink manzanilla; (g) trumpet and castanets (she plays the latter); (h) the mountains; (i) smugglers; (j) the bullfight.

62. (e): In *The Great Caruso* (1951), the singer was portrayed by Mario Lanza. Caruso appeared in a couple of silent films, but neither were autobiographical.

63. (a) Gloria; (b) Gibson; (c) gavotte; (d) *Gaspard de la nuit*; (e) Graham; (f) *Gradus ad Parnassum*; (g) *Gioconda*; (h) Goldman; (i) Glinka; (j) Gold; (k) Gretel; (l) Gypsy; (m) Goldberg; (n) Gilda; (o) "Ghost"; (p) Giulietta; (q) ground; (r) Guglielmo; (s) Garden; (t) Gluck; (u) Gunther; (v) Gould; (w) Glass; (x) *Giselle* (one *l* for Ms. MacKenzie); (y) Greenhouse; (z) Grove.

64. (b): *Nabucco* was written by Verdi.

65. (a) 2; (b) 8; (c) 4; (d) 1; (e) 6; (f) 7; (g) 5; (h) 3.

66. (a) *Aida*; (b) *Rigoletto*; (c) *Otello* and *Falstaff*; (d) *Un ballo in maschera*; (e) *La forza del destino*.

67a. (a) 2; (b) 4; (c) 1; (d) 3; (e) 5.

67b. She smokes. Whenever Gil enters their home, the place reeks of tobacco. As a result, he insists that Suzanne must be receiving a visitor who can only be a man.

68. (c).

69. (a) *Salome* by Richard Strauss; (b) *Tannhäuser* by Richard Wagner; (c) *Die Walküre* by Wagner; (d) *Die Meistersinger* by Wagner; (e) *Il trovatore* by Verdi; (f) *Prince Igor* by Borodin; (g) *Boris Godounov* by Mussorgsky; (h) *Lakmé* by Delibes.

70. The Jewel Song, The Ballad of the King of Thule, The Soldiers' Chorus, The Chorus of Swords, The Song of the Rat, The Song of the Golden Calf, The Drinking Chorus, The Spinning Wheel Song, Mephistopheles's Serenade.

71. Jean-Baptiste Lully.

72. (a) *La forza del destino*; (b) *Faust*; (c) *Faust*; (d) *Il trovatore*; (e) *Louise*.

73. (a) 5; (b) 6; (c) 4; (d) 11; (e) 1; (f) 10; (g) 8; (h) 7; (i) 9; (j) 2; (k) 3.

74. (a) Samuel Ramey, a bass, would not be cast to sing Don José, a tenor role. (b) Enrico Caruso, a tenor would not be cast to sing Rigoletto, a baritone role. (c) Jenny Lind was not singing anywhere in 1897, having passed away in 1886. She gave her last performance on an operatic stage in 1849. (d) The year 1946 is a bit early for Birgit Nilsson to have sung in the United States. She made her American début in 1956 and her bow at the Met three years later. (e) Jussi Bjoerling could not have sung in 1972; he passed away in 1960.

75. (a) Gian Carlo Menotti; (b) Douglas Moore; (c) Virgil Thomson; (d) John Corigliano; (e) Deems Taylor; (f) John Adams; (g) George Gershwin; (h) Samuel Barber.

SOURCES

Abdul, Raoul. *Blacks in Classical Music*. New York: Dodd, Mead, 1977.

Albani, Emma. *Forty Years of Song*. London: Mills & Boon, 1911.

Alda, Frances. *Men, Women, and Tenors*. Boston: Houghton Mifflin, 1937.

Antheil, George. *Bad Boy of Music*. Garden City, NY: Doubleday, 1945.

Arditi, Luigi. *My Reminiscences*. New York: Dodd, Mead, 1896.

Atkins, Harold, and Archie Newman. *Beecham Stories*. London: Robson, 1978.

Baker's Biographical Dictionary of Musicians. 7th and 8th eds. Edited by Nicolas Slonimsky. New York: Schirmer Books, 1984, 1992.

Bing, Sir Rudolf. *A Knight at the Opera*. New York: Putnam, 1981.

_____. *5000 Nights at the Opera*. Garden City, N.Y.: Doubleday, 1972.

Bispham, David. *A Quaker Singer's Recollections*. New York: Macmillan, 1920.

Bookspan, Martin, and Ross Yockey. *Zubin*. New York: Harper & Row, 1978.

Boosey, William. *Fifty Years of Music*. London: E. Benn, 1931.

Briggs, John. *Leonard Bernstein*. Cleveland: World, 1961.

Bushnell, Howard. *Maria Malibran*. University Park: Pennsylvania State University Press, 1979.

Calvé, Emma. *My Life*. New York: D. Appleton, 1922.

Casals, Pablo. *Joys and Sorrows*. New York: Simon and Schuster, 1974.

Chorley, Henry F. *Music and Manners in France and Germany*. London: Longman, Brown, Green, and Longmans, 1844.

Clemens, Clara. *My Husband Gabrilowitsch*. New York: Harper & Brothers, 1938.

Cohen, Aaron I. *International Encyclopedia of Women Composers*. 2d ed. 2 vols. New York: Books & Music, 1987.

Cross, Milton. *The New Milton Cross Complete Stories of the Great Operas*. Garden City, N.Y.: Doubleday, 1955.

Curtiss, Mina. *Bizet and His World*. New York: Knopf, 1958.

Cushing, Mary Watkins. *The Rainbow Bridge*. New York: Putnam, 1954.

179

Damrosch, Walter. *My Musical Life*. New York: Scribner, 1923.

Daniel, Oliver. *Stokowski*. New York: Dodd, Mead, 1982.

Del Mar, Norman. *Richard Strauss: A Critical Commentary of his Life and Work*. 3 vols. London: Barrie & Rockliff, 1962, 1968, 1975.

Dickson, Harry Ellis. *Gentlemen, More Dolce, Please!* Boston: Beacon Press, 1969.

Ewen, David. *Musicians since 1900*. New York: H. W. Wilson, 1978.

Farrar, Geraldine. *Such Sweet Compulsion*. New York: Greystone, 1938.

Fenby, Eric. *Delius as I Knew Him*. London: G. Bell, 1936.

Green, Martyn. *Here's a How-De-Do*. New York: Norton, 1952.

Gigli, Beniamino. *The Memoirs of Beniamino Gigli*. London: Cassell, 1957.

Gottschalk, Louis Moreau. *Note of a Pianist*. New York: Knopf, 1964.

Gotwals, Vernon. *Haydn: Two Contemporary Portraits*. Madison: University of Wisconsin Press, 1968.

Hauk, Minnie. *Memories of a Singer*. London: A. M. Philpot, 1925.

Heinsheimer, Hans. *Fanfare for 2 Pigeons*. Garden City, N.Y.: Doubleday, 1952.

Herz, Henri. *My Travels in America*. Madison: State Historical Society of Wisconsin, 1963.

Hetherington, John. *Melba*. New York: Farrar, Straus & Giroux, 1968.

Howe, M. A. DeWolfe. *The Boston Symphony Orchestra, 1881-1931*. Boston: Houghton Mifflin, 1931.

Johnson, H. Earle. *Symphony Hall, Boston*. Boston: Little, Brown, 1950.

Key, Pierre. *John McCormack*. New York: Vienna House, 1973.

Kostelanetz, André. *Echoes*. New York: Harcourt Brace Jovanovich, 1981.

La Grange, Henry. *Mahler*. Garden City, N.Y.: Doubleday, 1973.

Lawton, Mary. *Schumann-Heink: The Last of the Titans*. New York: Macmillan, 1928.

Leinsdorf, Erich. *Cadenza*. Boston: Houghton Mifflin, 1976.

Levant, Oscar. *Memoirs of an Amnesiac*. New York: Putnam, 1965.

_____ . *The Unimportance of Being Oscar*. New York: Putnam, 1968.

Liberace. *Liberace*. New York: Putnam, 1973.

Liszt, Franz. "Letter of a Bachelor in Music." *The Musical World*, August 4, 1837, pp. 132-3.

Lochner, Louis. *Fritz Kreisler*. New York: Macmillan, 1950.

Lytton, Sir Henry. *Secrets of a Savoyard*. New York: Da Capo Press, 1980.

Mapleson, James. *The Mapleson Memoirs*. New York: Appleton-Century-Crofts, 1966.

Marchesi, Blanche. *A Singer's Pilgrimage*. New York: Arno, 1977.

Marchesi, Matilde. *Marchesi and Music*. New York: Harper & Brothers, 1898.

Maretzek, Max. *Crotchets and Quavers*. New York: Da Capo Press, 1966.

Melba, Nellie. *Melodies and Memories*. Garden City, N.Y.: Doubleday, 1928.

Menuhin, Yehudi. *Unfinished Journey*. New York: Knopf, 1976.

Merrill, Robert. *Between Acts*. New York: McGraw-Hill, 1976.

_____. *Once More from the Beginning*. New York: Macmillan, 1965.

Moore, Gerald. *Am I Too Loud?* New York: Macmillan, 1962.

Moore, Grace. *You're Only Human Once*. Garden City, N.Y.: Doubleday, Doran, 1944.

Nettl, Paul. *The Beethoven Encyclopedia*. New York: Philosophical Library, 1956.

The New Grove Dictionary of Music and Musicians. Edited by Stanley Sadie. 20 vols. London: Macmillan, 1980.

The New Kobbe's Complete Opera Book. Edited by the Earl of Harewood. New York: Putnam, 1976.

Newman, Ernest. *The Life of Richard Wagner*. 4 vols. New York: Knopf, 1933, 1937, 1941, 1946.

Noble, Helen. *Life with the Met*. New York: Putnam, 1954.

Pavarotti, Luciano. *Pavarotti: My Own Story*. Garden City, N.Y.: Doubleday, 1981.

Peerce, Jan. *Bluebird of Happiness*. New York: Harper & Row, 1976.

Piatigorsky, Gregor. *Cellist*. Garden City, N.Y.: Doubleday, 1965.

Reeves, Sims. *Sims Reeves*. London: Simpkin, Marshall, 1888.

Rubinstein, Arthur. *My Young Years*. New York: Knopf, 1973.

Ruttencutter, Helen Drees. *Previn*. New York: St. Martin's Press, 1985.

Santley, Charles. *Student and Singer*. New York: Macmillan, 1892.

Sargeant, Winthrop. *Geniuses, Goddesses, and People*. New York: Dutton, 1949.

Schonzeler, Hans-Hubert. *Bruckner*. New York: Grossman, 1970.

Schuh, Willi. *Richard Strauss*. New York: Cambridge University Press, 1982.

Seroff, Victor. *Serge Prokofiev*. New York: Funk & Wagnalls, 1968.

Sills, Beverly. *Bubbles*. Indianapolis: Bobbs-Merrill, 1976.

Slezak, Leo. *A Song of Motley*. New York: Arno, 1977.

Slezak, Walter. *What Time Is the Next Swan?* Garden City, N.Y.: Doubleday, 1962.

Slonimsky, Nicolas. *A Thing or Two about Music*. New York: Allen, Towne & Heath, 1948.

Smith, Moses. *Koussevitzky*. New York: Allen, Towne & Heath, 1947.

Spohr, Louis. *The Musical Journeys of Louis Spohr*. Edited by Henry Pleasants. Norman: University of Oklahoma Press, 1961.

Stassinopoulos, Arianna. *Maria Callas*. New York: Simon & Schuster, 1981.

Taubman, Howard. *Music on My Beat*. New York: Simon & Schuster, 1943.

Tiomkin, Dimitri, and Pierre Buranelli. *Please Don't Hate Me*. Garden City, N.Y.: Doubleday, 1959.

Toobin, Jerome. *Agitato*. New York: Viking, 1975.

Tromboners. New York: Knopf, 1932.

Tyson, Alan, and H.C. Robbins Landon. "Who Composed Haydn's Opus 3?" *The Musical Times*, July 1964, pp. 506-7.

Walker, Alan. *Franz Liszt*. New York: Knopf, 1983.

Willson, Meredith. *And There I Stood with My Piccolo*. Garden City, N.Y.: Doubleday, 1948.

──────────. *Eggs I Have Laid*. New York: Holt, 1955.

Winkler, Max. *A Penny from Heaven*. New York: Appleton-Century-Crofts, 1951.

Wroth, Warwick. *The London Pleasure Gardens of the Eighteenth Century*. London: Macmillan, 1896.